Bernard Wills

Why Believe

Essays on Religion, Rationality and Belief

MINKOWSKI
Institute Press

Bernard Wills
Humanities Program
Grenfell Campus
Memorial University of Newfoundland
Corner Brook, NL Canada A2H 6P9

Cover: Paul Gauguin, The Yellow Christ (`https://commons.wikimedia.org/wiki/File:Gauguin_Il_Cristo_giallo.jpg`)

ISBN: 978-1-927763-44-5 (softcover)
ISBN: 978-1-927763-45-2 (ebook)

Minkowski Institute Press
Montreal, Quebec, Canada
http://minkowskiinstitute.org/mip/

For information on all Minkowski Institute Press publications visit our website at http://minkowskiinstitute.org/mip/books/

CONTENTS

ii

1 INTRODUCTION

There has been a fair bit of popular discussion of religion in the past decade or so, some of it coarse in tone and spectacularly ill-educated in its subject matter. A style of secular humanist apologetics associated with people such as Richard Dawkins and Sam Harris (among others) has come to define much popular and even some educated discussion of religious belief. My point here is not to belabor the deficiencies of this apologetic as many thoughtful people have already taken Dawkins and Harris to task for their perceived crudities. I take it as established that none of these authors have done the necessary spadework to write usefully on religion. I will not, then, be engaged in any 'debunking' of Dawkins, Harris and their ilk except as it may serve as an occasion to illustrate the positive points I wish to make. At any rate, the discourse of 'new atheism' will continue to play a significant role in shaping public perceptions of religion whatever polemics are uttered against it. Indeed, a *Prospect* magazine poll has recently proclaimed Dawkins 'the world's leading thinker'! For good or ill Dawkins, Harris et. al. have become the popular and public face of the atheist humanism in the English-speaking world. No doubt this is becausethey freely and unapologetically promote an ideological stance that many more circumspect people may implicitly endorse: those who object to the style of Dawkins and Harris might well ask themselves whether, at the end of the day, they truly differ from them in substance. The polemics of Dawkins and Harris are grating: certainly, there are more nuanced voices. Yet their rigid empiricism and their grandiose sense of the place of science and technology in society are not alien to secular humanism at large which, let us remember, stands as a significant and permanent challenge to any and all religious discourse. It is this broader ideology that I want to address taking Dawkins, Harris, Pinker etc. in their proper role as starting points for the sort of nuanced discussion that has sometimes been far to seek. As I will explain further below, I believe that much popular and even some sophisticated atheism rests on mistaken assumptions about the nature of truth, rationality and belief.[1]

Nevertheless, articulating these assumptions and showing their limitations allows us to see the nature of truth and reason more clearly and to avoid pernicious dualisms that oppose scientific thinking to the humanities in general and to religion in particular. Science is neither as rational nor non-science as irrational as such thinkers like to pretend. In short, reason is a thing ill understood by many who proclaim their rationalism most loudly. The essays that follow will all make this point in various ways.

To begin though I will lay out my own basic attitudes on the subject of religion. I was, at one point in my life, a quite dogmatic atheist. Subsequently, I became quite dogmatically religious (without, alas, any change in my underlying personality). More recently, it has struck me with some force that God is indeed a God of love (and not piety) and so I have tried (I hope with some small success) to exchange religiosity for charity. Thus, the reader need engage in no nice speculation on my 'agenda'. My current position is simple: I contend that religious ideas, narratives, rituals, sacred texts and symbols belong as much as science, philosophy and the arts to the human patrimony and are (properly used) a source of consolation, wisdom and aesthetic delight of which we would be fools to deprive ourselves. Indeed, it

---

[1] I should make it clear that what I am referring to as 'atheism' here is not simple disbelief in God, which, after all, comes in too many varieties to count. By atheism I mean an organized and publicly visible ideology (influential in the Anglo-Saxon world) that combines disbelief in God with a number of other cognate moral, political and intellectual stances. These include A. a strict laicism in public affairs and education; B. a strong conception of human freedom and dignity as excluding any gods or god; C. a strong commitment to science and technology as keys to human flourishing; D. a progressive or 'Whig' interpretation of history which sees it as culminating in Western secular society and its culture of instrumental rationality; E. a marked tendency to 'scientism' or the view that scientific method constitutes the proper paradigm of knowing; F. strict naturalism which sees any and every concession to the 'supernatural' as a threat to the integrity of science; and G. a belief that Darwinian biology especially is the key to liberating human beings from enslavement to any conception of a deity or 'cosmic designer'. This book is not a refutation of this complex of ideas whose components work together affectively and morally as much as they do logically and so is on some level immune to rational critique. Rather, it is an invitation to consider that this particular ideology may not, as its supporters have it, be identical with reason as such. It goes without saying that Atheism as simple non-belief commits no one to any of the positions listed above.

seems evident to me that religions and their history are crucial to the self-understanding even of secular humanity: religion, along with philosophy and art is one of the basic modes in which humans have educated themselves in the fundamental tensions of existence and, as such, has been (and most likely will continue to be) basic to human flourishing. What is more, I think recognition of this fact is part and parcel of any educated view of the world regardless of whether one is a believer in any particular religion and irrespective of whether one believes in a deity. To understand ourselves is one of the basic tasks of the humane disciplines and this must involve a fair and accurate understanding of religion.

Now to my mind I have just uttered a string of banalities. Yet there is another discourse about religion (one which many take to be sophisticated and 'cutting edge') that seems violently opposed to everything I have just said. According to this discourse 'religion' or 'faith" is an inhuman other, a sub-rational, perhaps sub-personal 'virus of the mind' inherently hostile to science and other public standards of rationality and a fundamental threat to liberalism and democracy. When critics point out that religions like Christianity and Islam have a long tradition of disciplined rational discourse and express themselves in progressive as well as reactionary forms the response is that fundamentalism is the a-historical essence of religion as such and that these more liberal viewpoints represent the attenuation of a proper religious stance to the world. The easy retort to this judgment is that secular humanism (at least the aggressively doctrinaire sort we associate with the so called 'new atheists') can find nothing in the religious heritage of human kind but its fundamentalist other because it is itself a form of fundamentalism: its extreme (and philosophically untenable) empiricism is the precise counterpart of biblical literalism even as its zealotry (religious believers are not only wrong but culpably wrong if not actually insane) carries forward the tired tradition of sectarian contempt. One is hardly surprised when a check of the internet reveals that there are humanist associations that maintain Sunday services and that 'the saved' often testify to each other by means of 'conversion stories'!

Of course, my opponents will not see it this way. In their mind they are simply asserting robust common sense. When an honest man says the world was created in six days, he means nothing more and nothing less than that the world was created in six days. Religion, in other words, is a set of factual empirical propositions which can be confirmed, disconfirmed, or judged more or less likely in light of

4

our knowledge of the laws of nature. Of course many assert that religious beliefs are no such thing; for instance, it is pointed out that many of them have a metaphorical or symbolic import. Alas, many secular humanists will snort in derision at this, suspecting a trick. They know in their bones that in the bad old days Zeus was thunder and Poseidon water. Yet now that we know thunder is an electrostatic discharge and water is H_2O it seems plain as day that these ancient beliefs were mistaken. However, 'religious liberals' refuse to accept the obvious and invent new 'symbolic' meanings for things they no longer actually believe. They invent a kind of belief that no one had any inkling of or need for until science showed the empirical claims of religion to be vacuous. Fundamentalists, at least, are honest in this regard and at one with secular humanism in holding these liberal sophisticates in particular contempt. What we need most of all is an honest confrontation between 'genuine' literal religion and the 'facts' uncovered by science; a confrontation which can end only with the complete rout of all religious beliefs.

I suppose some of this is an understandable reaction to the post 9/11 world. Anglo-Saxon elites have long claimed leadership of the globe as bearers of liberalism, technology, science and the other grand ideals of the enlightenment. However, reaction breeds reaction. When this hegemony is challenged (with some success) by internal and external 'proletariats' the temptation is very strong to respond with an arrogant and exclusive assertion of the values associated with instrumental rationality and Western technocracy. Yet here is why this new discourse (and its evident popularity) is somewhat disturbing to a teacher of the Humanities. Few atheists extend their critique of religion to a critique of the liberal arts as well; their self-image as members of the cultural elite would seem to preclude too violent an assault on music, poetry and fiction.[2] Few people, after all, wish to ap-

---

[2]In a refreshing display of candor Dr. Alex Rosenberg does not shrink from this conclusion. In his book *The Atheist's Guide to Reality* he states: "When it comes to ways of knowing, scientism must plead guilty to the charges of hegemonic ambition. There is only one way to acquire knowledge, and science's way is it... it cannot therefore accommodate the humanities as disciplines of inquiry, domains of knowledge." (p. 306) We may contrast Rosenberg's claims with those of Larry Lauden who suggests that we should not worry about whether our beliefs are scientific (or pseudo-scientific) so much as whether our beliefs are, in some broader sense, warranted. This may involve abandoning the belief that scientific procedures involve some special and privileged kind of warrant. In Laudan's view many of the beliefs of football coaches or carpenters have more warrant than those of orthodox scientists. (see Lauden, 1983) What follows in this book is in line with the pluralism

pear nakedly philistine. However, the positivistic bias of much Secular Humanist discourse would, if thought through to its conclusion, hardly offer a strong position from which to value the intuitions of poets, visual artists and composers. If the threat of fundamentalist religion is to be countered by a violent assertion of the hegemony of instrumental reason where does this leave literature or philosophy? Keats' equation of truth and beauty hardly gives us any more purchase on empirical reality than belief in the burning bush. Nor does his famous ode make much sense as a collection of literal propositions about an urn. Is poetry and myth then to be confined to the realm of the subjective: a matter merely of taste and feeling perhaps, private emotion but not knowledge or truth? What place could it possibly have beyond the realm of private appreciation? The Secular Humanist is here faced with a fork: if the problem with religion is that it cannot justify its claims by experimental evidence then this condemnation would entail evacuating most of the humane disciplines of cognitive legitimacy. Conversely, if the humanities have their *own* special modes of knowing then scientific standards of understanding cannot, without further ado, be taken as rendering all religious claims false or meaningless: it may well be, for instance, that religious beliefs can be intelligently justified in a manner more comparable, say, to the learned judgments of scholars or art critics.

Of course, it could well be that we do *not* need poetry or philosophy to comprehend the world and that they along with all other non-scientific discourses are essentially forms of recreation, necessary only for those whose dreamy minds are ill-equipped to withstand the rigors of science. The following book will attempt to show that this is not the case and that the attitude outlined above is as fundamentally mistaken about religion as it is about science itself. To put my case briefly, I believe the notion of fact appealed to by both scientism and fundamentalism is a late abstraction: religion is in its origin and essence a *symbolic* discourse. Thus, the identification of religion properly speaking with fundamentalism is mistaken. Secondly, I hold that the symbolic is a valid order or form of knowing and that judged by standards appropriate to them religions can be shown to be rich in genuine cognitive content. Thirdly, I hold that there can be intelligent justifications for choosing to adopt a particular religious stance

---

suggested by Lauden:.if scientism is true than the humanities are not domains of knowledge. However, the humanities are domains of knowledge. Therefore, scientism is untrue.

if justification is understood broadly (as it is in the humanities) and not in terms of a puritanically narrow scientific rationalism. Finally, I hold that confronting the positivist critique of religion allows us to see more clearly the nature of reason and justification in the Humanities and goes some way towards justifying the humane disciplines as having their own intellectual discipline *not* reducible to those of the sciences.

Below I shall argue that religion is something that cannot be wished away for humans are symbolic animals and religion is the primary pre-reflective mode in which we picture to ourselves some whole which provides a meaningful context for our actions and reflections. The following essays will, I hope, establish the importance of the symbolic imagination and the interpretive practices of those who elicit *readings* from it as a necessary complement to the interpretation of nature in the sciences. The result of this will be, I hope, a clearer conception of the nature of religious beliefs which will distinguish a humane understanding of them from those positivistic distortions (both secular humanist and fundamentalist) which block us from grasping their true significance. Understanding religious discourse as an exercise in representative imagination frees us from the slavish idolatry of external fact which underwrites triumphalism of either sort. Religion is not in competition or conflict with other domains of activity. In short, I will attempt to outline a humane understanding of religion both for its cultured (or not so cultured) despisers *and* for those whose conception of the demands of piety entails the assertion of all that is most particularistic in their respective traditions. Thus, it is my aim that both doctrinaire secularism and aggressive religiosity may find some correction and moderation in the following pages.

With this aim in mind I offer the following essays for the reader's consideration. As my chief focus I have chosen the problems of rationality, knowledge and belief and for this reason I have addressed essays to Richard Dawkins, Sam Harris and Steven Pinker. These authors stress the epistemological implications of religious belief which is also my principle focus in these essays. Accordingly I have included essays on the non-propositional character of religious language, the existence of God, the role of theological discourse and the nature and legitimacy of belief. I conclude the book with two shorter essays on the relationship between religion and the enlightenment and the nature of religious truth. Reading these essays will allow the reader to distinguish between justification as it operates in the sciences and the less formalized procedures used in the humanities in general and religion in particular. The reader will also learn to appreciate that there are different levels of precision appropriate for different inquiries. The result will be an epistemological pluralism that allows for a variety of modes of knowing and a plurality of possible perspectives. For the sake of the general reader I have tried to keep technical discussion to a minimum. I have however made some recommendations in the footnotes for readers who wish to explore some of the issues I raise more deeply.

8

2 THE ZEUS DELUSION

> *"The wise is one alone: it is willing and unwilling*
> *to be called by the name of Zeus."*
> (Heraclitus, fragment 27.)

I

I believe it was Richard Dawkins who first issued the following challenge to the Monotheists of this world: you are an Atheist about all the Gods of other religions, why not go one further?[3] Somewhat later, listening to a colleague speak on the necessity of Atheism I heard another version of this claim: Atheism about most gods is the de facto position of most people most of the time! After all, he challenged his audience, are you not all Atheists about Zeus? Since then, I have encountered this question a number of other times: indeed, it now seems an established trope characteristic of a certain sort of dogmatic Atheist. What I thought was a throwaway line in a popular author seemed now to have grown some legs: attaining the status perhaps of what certain people would call a 'meme'. What is more, it seemed to me that there was something worth examining here: if there is one thing in this world of which I am convinced it is that I am NOT an Atheist about Zeus in spite of the fact that I offer him no fatted calves and interact with him almost entirely as a character in some of my favorite poems and plays. But why exactly does it strike me as bizarre to say that I am a non-believer in Zeus? What in fact does it mean to say that I am a non-believer in something? What is it, in fact, to hold a belief? When I say that Dawkins believes in evolution, that Obama believes in the constitution, that Rousseau believed in the

---

[3]Richard Dawkins, *The God Delusion* (Boston: Houghton Mifflin Co., 2006), 53.

state of nature, that an Orthodox Christian believes the Virgin Mary is present in an icon and that my neighbor believes her cat is indoors am I using the word in the same sense each time?[4]

My position, which I will argue by using the question of Zeus as a kind of test case, is that in fact there are a number of incommensurate kinds or orders of belief and that Dawkins' question is founded on what philosophers call a category mistake: Dawkins and his cohorts deny the existence of Zeus in a sense that I (and I suspect an Ancient Greek as well) would regard as strictly secondary. In explaining what I mean by this I hope to illustrate the difference between truth in the propositional sense and what I would call truth in representation or paradigmatic truth. In other words, I hold that there can be truths that cannot be expressed adequately in the propositional language of empirical fact and that mythology and religion contain a high proportion of such truths. For this reason I hold that religious and mythological traditions can be perfectly reasonable objects of belief and that there is nothing at all ridiculous or strange about placing the Olympian gods somewhere on the continuum of one's beliefs.

Now I should be clear on one point: belief is not necessarily the only form in which religious wisdom can be possessed. Much of the history of Western (and I suppose Eastern) religions is taken up with attempts to overcome the limits of representation through conceptual thought (as in philosophical theology) or direct experience (as in mysticism). Faith, as the medieval philosophers held, seeks understanding. However, this essay is not an exercise in speculative theology or mysticism, regardless of how valuable those two endeavors might be. It is more directly concerned with the rationality or irrationality of beliefs for an idea reasonable in itself need not be held in an explicitly rational form: religion is a realm of *implicit* mind so that conceptual content is often displaced into representational schemes which are inhabited more than they are directly reflected upon and given tacit credence more than they are demonstrated or argued for. My thesis is that openness to mythic or religious discourse does not involve us in

---

[4]If I believe *that* the cat is indoors this is very different that believing *in* the constitution. In the first case I believe the proposition 'the cat is indoors' should map onto the world in some way. In the second I believe it is the world that should map onto the constitution. It would be very strange, for instance, to say that the fact that women cannot vote in Saudi Arabia is a falsifying instance of the U.N Declaration of Human rights. Clearly then there are at least two different senses in which we use the word belief. Below we will see that in fact there are many more.

a general abandonment of intelligence as is often assumed. As there is representative truth there is also *truth in representation* and this I claim can be assessed in an act of interpretive judgment regardless of whether it can be confirmed or disconfirmed by direct observation. Moreover, judgments concerning which belief system I ought to adhere to are, like judgments in literary criticism or art, often highly individuated; they often attain not to universal or necessary truths which hold for all subjects whatsoever but to *personal* or *subjective* truths. In this they resemble judgment in fields like literary criticism: one may have a well-considered judgment on the meaning of *Romeo and Juliet*, indeed, one may have a deep comprehension of that play, but that does not preclude another well-considered judgment differing from yours. I will expand on this comparison below. However, for now I simply want to note that these essays articulate a kind of *pragmatics of belief* rather than a quest for ultimate certainties. Partly, of course, this reflects what I think it is within my modest talents to accomplish. More fundamentally though, I hold any absolutist discourse to be problematic for the (at present) irreducibly pluralist global society we inhabit. Accordingly, I will attempt to show how religious and mythical conceptions can be among our reasonable beliefs while allowing for a fundamental plurality of perspectives.

To begin, I will discuss the question of belief as it pertains to figures like the Olympian gods. What does it mean to believe (or not) in Zeus? Here is one possible theory: to believe in Zeus is to assent to a proposition: there is an x such that that x is Zeus, husband of Hera, father of Athena, son of Chronos, king of all the Gods, etc. To disbelieve in Zeus is to deny such a proposition. Crucially, a proposition of this sort is one we tend to accept or reject on evidentiary grounds. So, if I say I believe in Zeus it means I believe there is an instance of the description 'son of Cronos'. What is more, it is often assumed that the reason I hold this belief is that some observation or inference from an observation serves to confirm it. It is then very easy for Mr. Dawkins (or anyone else of his persuasion) to claim that the 'evidence' for the existence of Zeus is as thin as that for mermaids and unicorns and that if I am not willing to call myself a Zeus Atheist I must be some rare species of fool. Well, this point of view is eminently sensible, so much so that it might seem sheer mystification to deny it. However, I can identify at least three problems with viewing the existence or non-existence of Zeus in these terms. Explaining these problems will perhaps shed some light on the question with which we began: what does it mean to have a belief? I am not sure I can give a comprehensive positive answer but I can at least give something of a negative one: though beliefs can have a propositional element to them they cannot be reduced to that propositional element nor can the propositional element stand by itself without the others. To say 'there is an x such that that x is the son of Chronos' is to say many other things at the same time not all of which can be expressed in the same form. Beliefs of a propositional kind exist in a kind of field containing pre and supra propositional elements and cannot be separated from these fields except by a sort of abstraction.[5] So, on to my three objections.

The first and most glaring objection is that it is far from clear that the Ancient Greeks themselves believed or disbelieved in Zeus in this sense. [6] This is because few, if any, of the Ancients singled out the strictly propositional content of their religions from the affective,

---

[5]By 'pre-propositional' I refer to the 'tacit' or implicit beliefs that underlie and enfold our consciously enunciated 'propositional' knowledge. Often such tacit knowledge can be held in the form of myth, legend, custom, foundational metaphor, moral intuition, common sense, etc. I take it as established that our propositional knowledge depends at every point on a web of such tacit beliefs. By 'supra-propositional' I refer to that aspect of our belief or knowledge that runs always ahead of conceptual formulation: one is never done interpreting the significance of a figure like Odysseus or Hamlet; one is never done thinking about the existence and nature of God. Something of these things is always in excess of what we can at any given time consciously formulate. In fact, there are any number of reasonable beliefs that do not depend on factual, propositional truth. There are pragmatic beliefs (such as the belief that a cancer patient will beat her illness or that my partner is faithful), theoretical beliefs (theories and models in science are never simple pictures of 'the facts' but justify themselves in terms of fundamental intellectual values such as coherence or fruitfulness), symbolic-poetic beliefs (belief in the real presence say, or more generally, a belief that the plenitude or power of the symbolized dwells in the symbol), and finally, one might add as well moral or metaphysical beliefs which are not statements of facts (which might be otherwise) but statements about the value, significance or nature of the whole or totality which forms the ultimate context of our statements of fact (that humans and primates share crucial features in common is for many a fact that finds meaning in the theory that they share a common ancestry in a 'whole' that is through and through material). Clarifying different sorts of belief and how they interact can go a long way in clarifying confusion about the differing claims of science and religion though that goes beyond the scope of this essay. The classic source on tacit belief is, of course, Polanyi's *The Tacit Dimension* though the notion is surely as old as Plato.

[6]Many people have made this point but David C. Lindberg puts it very succinctly: "Our highly developed conceptions of truth and the criteria that a claim must satisfy in order to be judged true (internal coherence, for example, or correspondence with an external reality) do not generally exist in oral cultures and, if explained to a member of an oral culture, would probably seem quite useless". (*The Beginnings of Western Science* , p.11)

practical, cultural and symbolical dimensions. Rather, to believe in Zeus seems to have meant all these things at once in no particular order. Retrospectively, we might abstract a propositional element from their beliefs but there is little or no evidence that they held all these other elements to rest on the truth of a proposition: so much so that among the later Romans it seems to have been perfectly possible to be a philosophical 'non-believer' and a perfectly sincere worshiper of Rome's Gods. Also, Plato and Aristotle often speak of the gods in plural, and even use the names of the gods on occasion in spite of the fact that they were (at the very same time) sharp critics of the religion of the poets. Thus, it seems that the Ancients themselves did not attach a straightforward propositional sense to their statements about the gods such that questions like 'did Aristotle or Plato believe in Zeus?' have no simple answer. If this was not a simple question even for the Ancients there is no reason to think that it is a simpler question for us. Thus, it seems as if a conception of religious belief that seems obvious, indeed self-evident to us was not so to an ancient culture of great sophistication. Unless we wish to be parochial in our thinking we might do well to stop and consider whether this difference represents a limitation of the Ancients or of ourselves. If we do this it seems two further problems emerge.

Let me explain the first of these: I definitely have a relationship to Zeus. When they were small, I read to my children the delightful *D'Aulaire's Book of Greek Myths*. We shared these stories, discussed them and joked about them until the figures of the ancient gods became like characters around the house. Like the protagonist in Ridley Scott's *Gladiator* I might indeed greet a statue of Jupiter by saying 'Hello old friend'. This might not be pious Jupiter worship in the full sense but it is more than nothing. It seems I can speak about Zeus as at very least having what St. Anselm calls existence 'in a mind' and that is to give him a certain low degree of objectivity: there are certain things I cannot conceive of Zeus as doing! Thus, there is, at one extreme, the inter-subjective reality of cultural symbols which take on a life of their own apart from individuals who carry or transmit that culture. Accordingly, one answer to the question 'does Zeus exist?' is surely 'yes, Zeus exists as part of the cultural heritage of any educated person of a European or North American background'. If I were to say 'Zeus will strike you!' most educated people would know exactly what I meant. Probably, they would have a picture of a bearded man brandishing a lightning bolt with a look of righteous indignation on his face.

This hardly seems a very impressive sort of existence though perhaps it is more robust than appears at first glance. As far as I can make out their meaning, my Secular Humanist colleagues are getting at something like this with their talk of 'memes' as real entities which are even said to have a sort of agency. However, this is only the tip of the iceberg. The conception of Zeus developed by the great tragedians Aeschylus and Sophocles seems to express something both profound and exhilarating. Indeed, it seems to me to express something profoundly true. It is not a brief or easy task to articulate why this is so. However, of one thing I am convinced: nothing of their achievement would be diminished in the least if a trip to the top of Olympus revealed nothing but rocks! If I had to give a rough account of it, I would make the following claim: through their representations of Zeus the Ancient Greek poets and tragedians expressed their profoundest intuitions about the nature of moral and political life in a way that is of permanent relevance and interest for it touches on the most fundamental tensions of human existence. The name 'Zeus' summons for me, as for the Ancients, a whole constellation of thoughts and representations about fate, justice, and order of which the anthropomorphic figure forms a negligible part. Indeed, one might say that by the word Zeus I (and they) denote not an individual so much as an all-encompassing principle of order by which the tensions and oppositions of the world are held in a precise (if precarious!) balance. If I might borrow a phrase from Heraclitus, Zeus (as the tragedians come to conceive him) is a *logos* or intelligible principle that orders and constrains the flow of events in nature and society: if you like, he is the personification of the law-like necessity that constitutes the physical and moral universe. It therefore strikes me as an inept response to say that since no anthropomorphic entity matching Homer's description ever existed, I must necessarily be a Zeus Atheist.

Indeed, even for the Ancients the propositional notion of belief would founder on the fact that Dionysus is himself and any bottle of wine as well, and that Athena is both an individual agent and the city of Athens. Not only this, she is a statue, a character in the *Odyssey,* the prudence that stays Achilles' hand when he wishes to slay Agamemnon, prudence in general and a host of other things as well ranging from the most concrete to the most abstract. One might say that a god represents in one symbol the universal and particular at once, and thus seeks to encompass all at once and in a single poetic intuition levels of reality that reflective thought would tend to distinguish. One might say then that the Gods are concrete universals and to say that Athena exists is no more and no less than to say that prudence in general exists in and through specific instances of it, none of which by themselves exhaust what it means to be prudent. A God, if you like, is a Platonic form representing some fundamental principle or value like prudence, justice, the joy of intoxication, sexual desire or the productivity of the earth. Thus, to ask whether a God 'exists' is, in a sense, to ask whether people enjoy wine, want sex or act prudently: with the proviso of course that in the non-mechanistic figuration of the universe of the Ancients these phenomena will tend to be conceived as manifesting some irreducible quasi-personal force or power: in some sense they are self-instantiating principles.

A modern Western human being (such as I) is unlikely to conceive of Zeus or Athena with the full range of associations available to an Ancient Greek. I do not happen to think strongly about an individual agent or personal will when I think about Zeus though he has been memorably represented that way. Indeed, I scarcely think of him as a 'being' at all. Perhaps then I think that Zeus, though not real in a propositional sense, is a beautiful and comforting fiction? This strikes me as far too weak a description of my state of mind when I contemplate the conclusion of the *Oresteia*. It is even too weak a description of the gladiator greeting the statue of Jupiter. No, my attitude to Zeus seems to be that he is part of my world in a way that is utterly indifferent to whether I classify him as a fiction or as the real instantiation of a description. If he is not a fact then he is not less than a fact but more than one! There are fictions and then there are meaningful fictions: fictions that for whatever reason take on a life of their own. One might say that there are fictions which seem to have something 'true' about them, so much so that we are unsure whether fiction is the exact category for them. There may never have been two such people as the fisherman and his wife in Grimm's fairy tale but two truer human beings have perhaps never been depicted for they are, of course, all of us in our desiderative aspect. A beautiful or comforting fiction has, I propose, to be more than a simple fiction if it truly is beautiful and comforting. There must be something true about it and if that truth is not of a propositional kind then there must be some other sort of truth.

It seems then that there is an order of realities which are neither simple figments nor instances of descriptions and that the Ancient

Gods (in their representational aspect) along perhaps with great literary figure like Hamlet or Lear belong in this category. One can speak of them as existing more or less as one speaks of 'the spirit of the laws' or other representations that straddle the concrete and abstract at once. One's relationship to these entities is in considerable measure communal and practical and in holding this, I think, I am at one with what any Ancient Greek meant when he said he believed in Zeus (at however much lower a level of intensity!). These great 'symbols' or 'archetypes' are not facts *per se* (at times they may be literal nonsense) but are of an order of magnitude more significant than either facts or run of the mill fictions. Hamlet fascinates because on some level he expresses the plenitude of life more completely than we do on our dull, ordinary, empirical level: being larger than life he expresses more of it than any of us can know or instantiate at once. If I may put it this way, symbols are not things we see but things through which we see ourselves and the world around us, they are truth but truth in the form of paradigmatic representations. Apart from propositional truth there is symbolic or representative truth. There is an indwelling of the world in us in the mode of imaginative representation and this is what comes before us in the world's great myths and religious symbols. In this light, we might understand the surprising (to us) claim of Aristotle that poetry is more universal and closer to philosophy than history.[7]

Thus, the Olympian gods might be thought of as a representative ordering of the tension and relation of such phenomena as family, state, war, passion, reason, ecstasy, technology, nature and the like. Perhaps our figuration of nature as a 'kingdom' with 'laws' or as a 'machine' comes somewhat close to this: we do not quite believe this representation to be literally true (though it is not false either) but it is the master metaphor that guides our thinking about the natural world and we could not function without it. Zeus and his children are a representation but one that (if examined closely) are true to life so that they are not just a representation but embody in imaginative terms a genuine poetic intuition of cosmic order. As such, they have their own sort of truth for one cannot create just any pantheon of Gods any more than one can use just any metaphor about nature. No, 'true' depictions of the Gods like any great religious symbol unite in a single image a whole host of perceptions about social, political, moral, natural and spiritual phenomena: they are always about much

---

[7] *Poetics* 9, 5-10.

more than what they directly say.

I will use the following example to illustrate this point. I don't think anyone, even if they are Christian, loses much sleep over the question of whether they will be resurrected at the end of time with their hair, nails and genitals all intact. Yet anyone who reads what Thomas Aquinas writes on this question[8] can see that the 'literal' question is hardly what is important. St. Thomas is making a profound point about the dignity of the human person and its corporeal expression. It seems to me quite possible to say 'I believe I will be resurrected with my nails and hair' quite apart from any opinion I might have about what the end of the world will look like. This is even a practical point: anyone who decides to shame someone by forcibly shaving their head (as happened to collaborators in WWII) knows the truth of what Aquinas says in this passage. Even if Aquinas believed literally what he was saying about the end of the world (something certain stories about the end of his life might lead one to question) there is always a 'surplus' layer of significance to any mythic-religious symbol (like the notion of a general resurrection at the end of time). Thus, whatever propositional elements may be abstracted from religious expressions and images do not begin to exhaust their significance or even necessarily form their most important element. Often, their representative or paradigmatic value is as great or greater and this is surely why the Ancients did not strongly emphasize the propositional truth or falsity of their stories and images of the gods.

Perhaps one might object that the ambiguity I have pointed to about the status of propositional beliefs in religion is a peculiarity of Ancient religion. Maybe Moslems or Christians believe that 'there is an x such that that x is the God of Abraham, Isaac and Jacob' and that this commits them to believing that 'there is no x such that that x is Zeus, king of the gods'. Well, there are, no doubt, many Christians who would put it that way. An ontology such as that of Mr. Dawkins does seem to be a feature of religious fundamentalism as well; we might call it a metaphysics of fact. So, maybe the question is just 'aren't most contemporary religious people Atheists about all gods but one'? Well, perhaps they are, as I shall explain below, but I argue here this has little or nothing to do with assent to propositions. Firstly, I very much doubt that anybody believes in the literal existence of Adam and Eve and consequently finds the story of the fall meaningful and true. I am pretty much convinced that even for

---

[8] *Summa of Theology* Q. 80, art. 1-5.

fundamentalist believers it is the other way round: so meaningful and potent do they find the story (it is, to my mind, *the* story about self-consciousness, freedom and individuation) that, knowing of no higher grade of truth than literal fact , they attribute that form of reality to it. In this, I think, a believer in the literal truth of *Genesis* is very like the Ancient Greek who can think of no stronger way to express his intuition that a principle of just order governs events than to say that Justice is an anthropomorphic figure sitting on a mountaintop. Consequently, I would say that the fundamentalist Christian is making a category mistake by employing an ontology inadequate to express the true nature of his or her beliefs. However, I should point out that fundamentalist literalism (like the rejection of the 'literal image' by a certain sort of atheist) is a reflective and even rationalistic position: the truth of the complex and multifaceted image is self-consciously *judged* to lie primarily in its literal facticity (as opposed to some other category) and this distinguishes modern fundamentalism sharply from ancient Pagan or Christian religious sensibilities (for which the image in its implicit or pre-reflective mode encompasses all levels of meaning at once). [9]

But is there room in the Judeo-Christian-Islamic universe for stories or characters that are neither simple figments nor literal fact? Well, yes because according to the highest teachings about him God himself is neither a fiction nor a fact. This may sound surprising to the general reader but it is in fact strictest orthodoxy that God does not exist. In a tradition going back to Xenophanes at least, and carried on by all the great philosophers, mystics and theologians (Jewish, Islamic, Greek and Christian) it is said that God not only surpasses the mode of fiction in reality but also surpasses the mode of deter-

---

[9]Of course this is something Dawkins would vigorously deny. For him, non-literal conceptions of religious belief are appealed to only when the primary literal sense has failed. Once we realize that Zeus is not literal thunder we have lost the innocence of true religion and, by sleight of hand, attempt to paper over this loss by substituting a secondary discourse such as allegory or speculative theology which has no genuine relationship to the original religious phenomenon. This is what lies behind his persistent refusal to engage the theological tradition of which he remains, by his own admission, ignorant on principle: for him it is simply not religion (see below). This aggressive idolatry of literal fact is a trait he shares with his fundamentalist opponents but, alas, he fails to see that the literal propositional sense of a religious belief is as much an abstraction as the most rarified discourse of the theologian. What needs stressing against both these viewpoints is the necessity for human self- knowledge of a realm of symbolic and mythic discourse. Humans cannot begin with an empiricist version of plain speaking but only with image and symbol and narrative, as shall be argued below.

minate fact. In other words, God does not exist as a determinate x subject to representation by ordinary propositional logic. As Plato says 'The Good' or 'God' is *huperousias* or 'beyond being'.[10] Thus, God, as the supreme condition of all facts is not himself a fact but a mode of reality infinitely surpassing mere fact: when Aquinas says that god is not 'a being' but simply 'to be' or Descartes says that God is 'causa sui' or ground of his own existence this is what they are driving at. This is not to say that God is not 'real'. If I am a Christian I certainly recognize that agape or unconditional love manifests itself as the supreme ordering principle of my life. However this is not belief in a proposition of the form 'there is an x such that that x is supreme unconditional love'. Unconditional love is not subject to representation as an x to which I can attach the qualification of existing or not existing in the mode of finite entities. It is not pointed to like a black crow but experienced as a transformative power. It is not less but more real than the finite objects about which we utter true and false propositions. This, by the way, is what St. Anselm showed by his famous (and deeply misunderstood!) 'ontological argument'. Thus, metaphysical ultimates (like the Christian God, the Platonic Good, the Hindu Brahman), being between and behind all determinate oppositions, have something of the 'mediumistic' character of archetypes and paradigmatic figures: like Plato's sun they are not something seen but that through which we do the seeing. Certainly, the Christian God is not an entity whose existence precludes another entity called the son of Cronos. Thus, existence according the categories of ordinary propositional logic does not exhaust reality and is not adequate to express the meaning of mythic, poetic or theological language: indeed, God himself (if one believes in him) does not exist in the sense we ordinarily attach to the word exist.

Thus, religious beliefs differ from propositional beliefs as it were by excess; they have a plenitude that factual beliefs do not and this plenitude does not depend on our regarding them as facts but rather the reverse (we tend to regard them as facts because they are full of meaning). There is another way in which religious beliefs differ from ordinary propositional ones: they do not seem to be subject to the law of the excluded middle. All crows are black is either true or false but belief in Zeus is part of a continuum that may range from the most tenuous *pro forma* allegiance to a commitment that is total and unreserved. This is because a religious symbol can manifest

---

[10] *Republic* VI 509.

varying degrees of representative power and comprehensiveness and indeed, manifest these traits differently to different people. The Titan Prometheus may be an adequate representation of the power of craft-intelligence but to Aeschylus at least it is clear that Zeus is a more adequate representation of *the whole*. In turn, from the Christian perspective of the poet William Blake, the principle of cosmic order and justice represented by figures like Zeus or the watchmaker god of the deistic enlightenment is an image of nature unredeemed by the power of imagination, one whose potential for rigidity and violence is satirized in the figure of the debased tyrant Urizen. Even if I am not a Zeus worshipper I may well hold whatever was represented in the image of Zeus as an aspect of some more comprehensive symbol, as indeed Blake did by including Urizen (and thus reason and order) among his four 'Zoas', the 'living creatures' who represent the fullness of the divine humanity of Jesus.

Thus, my third objection is that religious beliefs rarely if ever express either/or propositions. One way to get at this is to ask what it might mean to not believe in Zeus. Does it always make sense to ask whether I disbelieve in something? I do not think that it does. I am almost certainly not an Atheist about Thor or Wotan because there is no practical context in my life in which it is meaningful to express my belief or disbelief in them. Not even Wagner's operas (which I love!) can make them real enough presences for me to even accept or reject. Nor is there any temple of Thor for me not to attend. I cannot define myself existentially by how I stand in relation to Baldur or Fricka. To a very large degree this is a personal accident. If I lived in Sweden the statement 'I don't believe in Thor' might well mean something: it might mean that I reject as fascist a certain sort of nationalism that decks itself out in neo- Pagan symbols (it is a striking fact that however fascinating the Norse Gods are in their literary context only the very wickedest of us have contemplated their revival). If the bare proposition 'I don't believe in an x such that that x is Baldur' is inadequate to express what it means not to believe in Baldur then it seems that belief as much as disbelief requires some life context over and above its bare propositional sense to be an object of meaningful negation or assent. Many beliefs do not have such a context for me so that I can neither affirm nor deny them. The most likely response of a !Kung hunter to a Westerner who told him the earth was round would be a shrug of indifference, for the proposition would relate itself to no practical aspect of his world and fit in none of his interpretive schemes.

Now certainly there is no temple of Zeus in Corner Brook to absent myself from. Still, it does not seem to me the case that the son of Chronos is in quite the same condition with me as Thor or Baldur. Indeed, this is true of the Olympian Gods in general. Their articulation into different functions still says something to me about the order of the world. It still seems natural to me to invoke Ares and Aphrodite when I want to say something about the mysterious co-inherence of love and strife. Indeed, to some degree I need Ares and Aphrodite to speak about it for 'love' and 'strife' are conceptual abstractions that stand in the place of things that are all too concrete and real. In some sense I need the language of the Gods to express the full force of what I want to say: 'ocean' says much less to me than 'Poseidon'. This is because speaking of the gods captures that aspect of living totality or wholeness in things which our analytic intelligence cannot reduce or dispel. Of course this is all at a much lower level of intensity than a pious Greek. There is along with my need an air of wistful affectation in my references to the Gods!

However, this seems to me something more than sheer non-belief even if it is much less than what I mean when I say that Jesus of Nazareth is the son of God. Sheer non-belief would mean that I in some sense reject Zeus and all he stands for. If I thought, for instance, that there was some deep and inviolable gulf separating biblical religion from the culture of classical antiquity I might throw all my Aeschylus in the trash or at least keep him around as a purely negative example. Then I would truly be an atheist about Zeus. So, do I believe in Zeus? Not in the sense that he is my primary religious symbol. Still, he is not so impotent a symbol either that I would put him nowhere on the continuum of my beliefs. This makes little sense on the propositional model of belief. Still, it seems to me so evident a fact that some more holistic account of belief seems necessary to describe it.

Perhaps I might call on the early Christians to help me out. The Apostle's creed, for example, begins with the statement 'I believe in God the Father, maker of heaven and earth'. It says 'believe in'. It does not say 'I believe that God the Father is the maker of heaven and earth' and the Patristic Scholars inform us that this phrasing is exact and intentional.[11] To believe in something is not to assert a fact about the world but to take an interpretive stance towards the facts.

---

[11] Alister McGrath, *Introduction to* Christianity (Oxford: Blackwell Publishers, 1997), 151-154.

To believe in God the Father is (rightly or wrongly) to see creation (and human history along with it) as benevolently providential despite all appearances to the contrary. To believe in Jesus Christ is to believe that the life and death of Jesus of Nazareth is a uniquely powerful demonstration of this fact. Neither of these claims is reducible to its propositional sense. As we have already seen, to say that God 'is' is always to some degree a manhandling of language. Really, it is what we must say instead of what we would really like to say but cannot. Our language has no conceptual structure adequate to the infinite mode of God's reality for, as John Scotus Eriugena (among many others) points out, what we mean by 'is' is existence according to one or several of the 10 categories (which don't apply to the simple reality of God).[12] Further, the assertion that Jesus is the son of God is one that could be affirmed or denied by two people in possession of the exact same set of biographical facts concerning Yeshua ben Yosuf from Nazareth. It is not a factual claim but a claim that a certain set of facts manifests a certain character, i.e. they reveal that God is Love in a unique and unsurpassable way. If certain ontological claims (of a metaphysical kind) about the man Jesus of Nazareth follow from this (as they do in the debates on Christology from the 4th and 5th centuries) it is only by way of a 'secondary' reflection.[13] The primary

---

[12] *Periphyseon* Book I, 460-461.

[13] By secondary I do not mean secondary in importance but in time. Faith is not reflection, it is more primary and immediate than that, but faith that is humanly (as opposed to inhumanly) lived will take on a reflective dimension. For example, a Christian, through the acceptance of Jesus as mediator between humanity and god, experiences salvation, or a lively sensation of rightness or at-oneness with the world. Her primary stance is that agape, or self-giving love, as exemplified by Jesus makes one a member of the kingdom and puts one at rights with both god and neighbor. This stance may, at first, be barely reflective: a free decision see god in the least lovable of our neighbors rather than the conclusion of an argument. However, as her intellect is engaged over time the believer may begin to perceive that certain quite determinate judgments follow from her interpretive stance: her faith may begin to express itself in doctrines that make claims of an apparently realistic character. In the beginning, she experiences Jesus as the one true mediator, at the end of the reflective stage she may judge that he is a human nature united hypostatically with the second person of the Trinity. A self-critical and intelligent faith depends on this reflective moment though the reflection in turn rests on the immediacy of the primary stance. Also, failures at this reflective level may (or may not) put the primary stance into doubt leading to a diminution of faith in it or the abandonment of the stance altogether. A good place to begin with the evolution of doctrine is *The Road to Nicea* by Bernard Lonergan, which gives a lucid account of the logic by which the doctrine of the trinity was formed. A broader introduction to this question is *The Emergence of the Catholic Tradition* by Jaroslav Pelikan.

stance of 'believing in' is a trust in and commitment to the notion that things are to be understood in a certain way and not others. Faith is a hermeneutic stance through and through. I should note though that hermeneutic stances are taken *towards* something so facts of a kind do play a role in religious systems. For instance, Orthodox Christianity assumes minimally that a man named Yeshua (or perhaps named something else?) lived and preached, in however rough-hewn a form, a doctrine of the Kingdom of God continuous with the religion that bears his name (I tend to think it assumes very little beyond this but others may differ). Naturally, if I happen to think Christian faith is a good hermeneutic stance overall I will look at the evidence for this factual minimum rather differently than someone who does not: what we are inclined to regard as plausible fact is heavily shaped by our world-view!

Thus, there seems to be a line we must draw between beliefs of a directly propositional character and religious beliefs. The latter are grounded in hermeneutic stances in a way the former are not (or rather are not so evidently) and that is why, while there may be a direct yes and no answer to the question of whether there is a tiger in the room there is no such answer for the question 'does Zeus exist'. This means that the question 'does Zeus exist' has in many contexts to be given a finely graded answer. If I were to answer this question for myself (I can answer it for no one else) I would say that, if by Zeus one means an irreducible principle of order that (however ambiguously) underwrites moral and political values of a basic kind I would say that Zeus is something I believe in (at least on a good day!) for I do act on the assumption that right and wrong matter to the universe in some more than contextual and purely contingent sense. However, insofar as I believe the image of a moral lawgiver is an incomplete vision of a deity in light of the Christian revelation of God as agape or self-giving love I would have to say that while I do not believe in less than Zeus I certainly believe in more. Some of what I believe as a Christian overlaps with what an Ancient Greek affirmed when he worshiped Zeus. This, we have seen, is because religious symbols have a surplus content over and above their propositional element which can be shared between one religious system and another and this means that no one can distinguish their religious commitments neatly in stark either/or propositions. To be a Christian is not at the same time to be a non-Olympian. I have no doubt that in an increasingly globalized society this is a point worth emphasizing.

II

No doubt none of this will please Mr. Dawkins and his supporters. They might happily consent to all I have said to this point and still be concerned that I have left the most important question of all completely out of account, and that is the question of evidence. They are right to be concerned. Just how am I to judge the truth of religious representations if not according to the methods of induction and deduction used in the sciences? And if religious statements *cannot* inherently be judged by such methods how can they be judged? How can we apply critical and reflective intelligence to beliefs of the kind laid out above? Does not the whole mode of myth and representation *exclude* criticism by replacing publicly observable 'neutral' facts with images and stories indifferent to confirmation or falsification by facts and events? Are myth and religion not thereby rendered *useless* and indeed a danger to public standards of rationality? Are they not a threat to the very foundations of science, technique and liberal democracy? Surely part of what it means to be enlightened and modern is to be a critical thinker able to question received wisdom and reflect critically on tradition. How can we do this unless we can subject the tales of poets and the utterances of prophets to rigorous methodical testing? If there are no tests that poets and prophets can meet what relationship do their words ever bear to 'objective' truth'?

As this seems to me a legitimate concern I will say a few words to address it. However at the outset I must make one thing clear: I will not be defending truth from myth and representation if by truth one means the bare correspondence of propositions to 'facts in the world'. I take the critique of the limitations of such a notion of truth by contemporary philosophers to be decisive. I also hold that there are more promising ways to defend the notion of intellectual responsibility. Thus, I will not be defending the 'public' realm of 'hard facts' against 'subjective belief' for I do not believe such a realm to exist. Bare propositional truth exists but only in the context of holistic webs of belief and it is these 'webs' taken as a whole that confer truth or falsity on distinct propositions. These interconnected systems of beliefs contain statements in the form of factual propositions but they contain as well moral, metaphysical, aesthetic and indeed theological conceptions, hunches, intuitions, customary beliefs, stock notions, narratives, master metaphors, traditions of practice etc. It is all these together and at once that constitute our world along with its 'facts': this is why world-views and foundational theories even in the sciences are notoriously resistant to 'falsification'.

There seem to me to be two consequences of this: firstly, that our most fundamental beliefs about the world constitute what I called above hermeneutic stances that are not and indeed cannot be simply 'read off' from the facts for there are no significant facts taken apart from them.[14] This is not to deny that there is an 'objective' 'out there world' that limits which hermeneutic stances can legitimately be taken. It is simply to state that 'things' cannot be isolated from frameworks of representation or hermeneutic stances and spoken of in themselves. Facts in science, for example, are mute without some (even very basic) theoretical construction: this is why theories are, in practice, measured against other theories and not against facts. As Paul K. Feyerabend points out, every interesting theory contradicts the facts at some point.[15] The crucial thing to point out about this is that the 'factual' pole of this dyad always underdetermines to some degree the 'interpretive' pole. This means that interpretive stances are of their nature highly individuated and depend as much on the values and priorities of the interpreter as on the thing interpreted. In short, there are in principle as many worlds as there are viable interpretive stances. I, for one, have no problem with the notion that while we inhabit a Judaeo-Christian Western 'nature' there may well be other 'natures' validly inhabited by other people.

Secondly, if there is in spite of the previous point real *confirmation* of our stances, this comes not from checking them against some neutral body of fact accessible independently of theory but progressively and pragmatically: belief systems justify themselves (or not) over time in terms of their power to generate theoretical insights both novel and gratifying as well as to produce a satisfying harmony of our interests and desires on a practical level. Conversely, belief systems fail when they stagnate or when they generate anomalies in precisely those areas where they were looked to for solutions (anomalies and problems, please note, accompany any theory or life stance and indeed are vital to how they function and progress; a theory without anomalies is a

---

[14]Dr. Ian Barbour states this point well by pointing out that in the realm of science "there is simply no theory free observational language... the selection of phenomena to study and the choice of variables considered significant to measure are theory dependent. The form of the questions we ask determines the kind of answers we receive. Theories are reflected in our assumptions about the operation of our equipment and in the language in which observations are reported."(*Religion in an Age of Science* (San Francisco, Harper and Row, 1990), 108).

[15]Paul K. Feyerabend, "How to Defend Society Against Science," *Full Poster* (2008), 222, http://www.fullposter.com/snippets.php?snippet=310

dead theory). Accordingly, any discussion of our religious or indeed scientific beliefs is in the context of an unfolding discussion of their adequacy in terms of fundamental intellectual, moral and aesthetic values.

Let me explain. When many people think of truth or falsity they think of confirming or disconfirming propositional statements. There are philosophical positions, such as *verificationism* and *falsificationism* which view truth in exactly this way.[16] Popular apologists for Atheism and Scientism often assume such a view of truth in their critiques of religious and mythic conceptions, insisting for instance that religious beliefs are 'without evidence' (by which they often mean observational or experimental evidence) or complaining that they are held tenaciously in the face of *disconfirming* evidence. There is no need for me to rehearse at length the difficulties of such a view of truth: they are well known though virtually ignored in popular apologetics. Suffice it to say that such a view ignores the extent to which our perceptual world is (and must be) our own active construction. To adopt an old adage: the thing known must be in the knower according to the mode of the knower. I would rather like to conclude by noting the difference between how hermeneutic stances are confirmed or disconfirmed and how the same process occurs with empirical propositions.

Take the example of an evangelical Christian who believes fervently in the resurrection of Christ. As far as I can tell there are no empirical

---

[16]So pervasive is a naïve version of scientific positivism in the apologetics of popular Atheism that the point must be emphasized that experimental verification in science is only one way of justifying a belief and cannot, in fact, function without the others. The first thing misunderstood by 'scientism' is science itself, which depends on a web of tacit beliefs which cannot of their nature be scientific. Reasonable motives for believing something can include: 1. Observation and experiment; 2. Custom or habit; 3. 'Know-how' or craft knowledge; 4. Interpretive judgment; 5. Intuition or intellectual insight; 6. Deduction; 7. Emotion and empathy; 8. Trust; 9. Affinity; 10. Moral and aesthetic judgment; and 11. Pragmatic imperatives. Testing a scientific theory by experiment can involve any or all of these other forms of justification. Moreover, any or all of these other forms can operate outside the context of science: indeed, they can in some select instances function better than science. I would consult a major league batting coach on how to hit a baseball before consulting a physicist. I would consult a loving dog owner on the emotional state of their dog before a zoologist (who, after all, is precluded qua zoologist from even attributing emotions to a dog). Thus, invidious contrasts between scientific knowledge and interpretive reasoning in the Humanities, say, or the emotive or affective knowledge of inter-personal relationships have no real foundation. Pace Dawkins and co., scientific reasoning offers a sort of knowing that may be perfectly valid in context but does not and, indeed, cannot represent the paradigm of knowledge as such.

facts that bear strongly on the question of whether or not Christ rose from the dead. I very much doubt whether there ever will or even could be such facts. However, it is equally apparent to me that the 'evidence' for such a belief is not really of this direct and immediate kind. There is no simple refutation or confirmation of the proposition "Christ rose from the dead" equivalent to the claim that there is a tiger in the room. For some this would be sufficient to consign any such belief to perdition. However, I would suggest that it is quite possible to evaluate such a belief if we regard it as a hermeneutical stance rather than as a factual claim. Religious beliefs, like aesthetic and moral ones come with their own *sui generis* sort of evidence which is to a large degree pragmatic and personal. The evangelical Christian who believes in the resurrection does so because it is a *saving* belief which sheds a transformative light on fundamental human concerns such as guilt, mortality and the problem of evil. The believer in the resurrection chooses to live her life in light of a species of hope which regards all negativity and evil as subordinate to the transfiguring power of *agape* or divine love. The test of this belief is the life she subsequently leads. Are her faculties of loving, perceiving, and relating strengthened or weakened by her Christian belief? Do her passions, interests and obligations fall into a more satisfying harmony? Or does she find herself more conflicted and inwardly torn? Do new insights open up to her as transformations once thought impossible occur before her eyes and problems that once seemed intractable fall away? Or does her stance seem fruitless, stagnant and productive only of rigid repetition and ennui? The difference between the evangelical who accepts the resurrection and the Atheist who rejects it has nothing to do with the fact that one appeals to evidence (or the lack thereof) and the other believes blindly: both of them are exercising the same type of interpretive judgment to different ends (i.e. there is no direct empirical confirmation or disconfirmation of Atheism or Christianity taken as a total life stance).

Of course this is not and cannot be a neutral public test. It cannot result in the knowledge of any and every neutral disengaged observer but only in the knowledge of a *person*. In this it resembles aesthetic judgment, the educated guesses of the historian or the intuitions of a legal scholar or philologist on how to resolve a delicate legal question or make a nuanced judgment on Homeric grammar. It is a belief grounded in what J.H. Newman termed our *illative sense*[17] and may

---

[17] John Henry Newman, *Essay in Aid of a Grammar of Assent.* (London: Burns

be freely accepted or freely rejected by anyone possessing the virtue of interpretive judgment. Truth grounded in a hermeneutic stance is in some sense *my* truth (and not someone else's). This is not to say that beliefs grounded in interpretive judgment remain (necessarily) purely private or subjective or that they preclude the exercise of intelligence operating by publically-shared standards. We live in history (inevitably) and interpretive stances like the Christian faith or the belief in the equality and freedom of persons are so woven in that history that they shape our perceptions and values whether we consciously wish them to or not: it is only in a abstract sense that as a citizen of Canada I can disbelieve in the equality of women; it is only in an abstract sense that I could reject Christianity for the religion of the ancient Hittites. I live inevitably within certain stances just by being born the person I am so that they have chosen objectivity for me beyond my discursive opinions and wishes. Nor does any of this preclude the possibility that in great theoretical constructions like quantum mechanics or evolutionary biology we can glimpse something of the truth. Certainly, thought through deeply and practiced extensively a philosophic, scientific or religious standpoint can take on an air of ineluctable necessity if it is sufficiently coherent and comprehensive of basic human concerns. However, I take it as established that my legitimate (though still personal) conviction that I have found the truth lays no necessity on anyone else to hold the same view in precisely the same form: an irreducible plurality of stances is both necessary and desirable because interpretive reasoning, as involving *pragmatic judgment*, has an irreducibly personal element. This seems to me the clearest way to reconcile intellectual responsibility with the demands of human liberty and the flourishing of individuality.

To return then to our original question, it seems evident to me that a belief in the representative truth of the Olympian religion is not an unreasonable one in spite of the fact that it is not open to empirical confirmation or disconfirmation in any straightforward sense: in this it resembles any of our other beliefs that are grounded in interpretive reasoning that adopts a stance *towards* the facts or chooses to *see as* rather than simply *see that*. What is more, I would assert that many, if by no means all, people of European descent and culture do have some level of belief in a divine necessity or providence such as an Ancient Greek might have represented by the figure of Zeus. Such people, of course, would nuance this belief very differently from Homer or

& Oates, 1881)

Hesiod under the influence perhaps of Hebraic or other traditions. The resemblance between their conception of providence and the classical pagan one may be here or there stronger or fainter; still, this does not seem to me in most instances to entail a blanket rejection of the classical pagan conception. To that extent it seems to me extreme to say that the default position of a contemporary Christian or Jew *must be* Zeus Atheism. Such a position is possible: one might argue that Hebraic and classical conceptions of divine order are in all respects contrary and incompatible. A follower of Swiss theologian Karl Barth might say something of this kind. However this is by no means an obvious or even an easy position to defend. It must be maintained with ingenuity and effort. For this reason, it seems necessary for me to conclude not only that I am not a Zeus Atheist but that I have some company in not being one.

3 THE INVISIBLE GARDENER

The following essay contains my proof of the existence of God. Many of my readers will find it very disappointing for it is not much of a proof. Indeed, the older I get the less interested I am in proving things, at least according to a certain conception of 'proof' that I have come to regard as dated. Both Atheists and many Christian apologists seem to me to share a common expectation about what should transpire in this essay. I am a believer in God. I am also a rational person (in general) with some training in philosophy and a couple of other academic disciplines. Surely if I *believe* something I have done the intellectually responsible thing and backed that belief up with some kind of argument. This argument should be of such a kind as to be persuasive to any and every observer who uses their reason in a neutral, detached and objective way. If my argument is a *good* argument it should persuade everybody who has the capacity to link a conclusion to its premises and can judge if it follows validly. If it does not, then there is either something wrong with my argument or with the person I am addressing it to. Surely this is what Anselm attempted to do in his famous 'ontological proof' and what Aquinas attempted in his 'five ways'. If I am to follow in their footsteps and persuade my readers that God exists surely I should either restate their arguments in such a form as to make belief in God an intellectual necessity for any and all disinterested subjects or offer some discursively rigorous proof on my own.

Actually, I am not so sure this *is* what the great philosophers mentioned above were attempting. The annals of ancient and medieval philosophy contain many chains of discursive reasoning whose conclusion is purported to be the existence of God. Yet discursive reason was always held to be a secondary and inferior thing to intellectual insight: the culmination of any proof was a flash of intuition into the eternity and necessity of the divine being. The philosopher enjoyed an actual (if limited) contemplation of God, not the abstract consideration of a conclusion, and the discursive steps of the proof were purely instrumental to this. Indeed, the intellectual assent was at the same time predicated on moral purgation of the will: God was not grasped as a living reality by the disengaged intellect but by the intellect and will of the whole person.[18] In our overtly rationalistic culture this process is almost certain to be misunderstood. Since this is so, I will not be presenting these ancient proofs in anything like their ancient forms. I *do* want to retain something of the ancient notion of an intellectual ascent to God but shorn of the appearance of objectifying rationalism with which moderns will inevitably take it. In other words, the ascent to God, if there is one, is a free movement of intelligence and love emanating from the core of the human person and not an external intellectual necessity that imposes an abstract deity as a conclusion of 'neutral' reason.

It is not as if an argument by itself is such a great thing: indeed, the most rigorous discursive proof conceivable is only a bit of cognitive dissonance if its conclusion does not fit with the rest of a person's outlook. This is especially so with respect to the question of God: as one student once put it to me, if reason leads to the conclusion that God exists then this is a motive for distrusting reason! Knowledge is holistic and personal and the student in question could find no place for a God in his constellation of values and thus rejected a proof he regarded as irrefutable in mere intellectual terms. My contention is that he was not entirely perverse in doing this: the mind, as J.H. Newman puts it, moves as a whole if it moves at all. Conversion may happen by an argument but only in a mind prepared to receive it in a myriad of subtle and implicit ways. Thus, an Atheist may formulate the problem of evil in a way that to him seems rhetorically and logically compelling and be surprised and annoyed to find his Christian friend going on exactly as he did before. Winning an argument rarely correlates with changing a mind! Even in the sciences (we now know thanks to the efforts of historians like Thomas Kuhn) anomalies and falsifying observations can pile up (in extreme cases) for centuries without producing a scientific revolution (absent a special motive to

---

[18]See Pico de la Mirandola, *Oration on the Dignity of Man*, Ch. 11-12, pp. 229-231, for a particularly eloquent account of this.

view the world in a new way). The impression sometimes created by philosophers of religion that the future of Christianity rests on the success of Smith's new theodicy or that the entire fate of Atheism hangs on refuting Jones' restatement of Barnes' third modal version of the ontological argument is surely a misleading one.

Still, without overrating discursive rationality too much it is not a great deal to ask of a professor of philosophy that he produce some intelligible account of what he believes and why, even if the answer he gives is not likely to be of an impersonal and universally necessitating kind. Such an answer to the question of God might, for all I know exist, but I do not here claim to possess it. Nor do I even claim to need it for the purpose of deciding the fundamental orientation of my existence; after all, we imprison people for life on grounds that fall far short of absolute certainty. In this spirit, I offer for the reader's consideration a rational reflection on the nature and grounds of my own theism. I do not offer this reflection because I think it an unusually enlightening or compelling account or because I think a religious autobiography of Bernard Wills will ever stand with Augustine or St. Theresa in the treasury of spiritual classics. My aim is alas more modest: for a certain sort of aggressive secularist all important questions are scientific questions answerable in terms of empirical evidence. Thus, answering the question of whether God exists involves deducing what consequences would follow from there being a God and checking those consequences against the data. To use a trite example, if it followed deductively from God's nature that the moon would be made of cream puffs it would be telling evidence against his existence if the moon turned out to be rock. One might even try to devise an experiment to test for the divine presence, say, by having people pray in a laboratory to see if their prayers were answered a statistically significant number of times. I do not think any case can be made for the existence of God in such terms. Nor do I think that if God existed his reality *would* be knowable by such means. However, reason need not operate in the formalized inductive manner set out above to arrive at intelligent conclusions about the world. Indeed, I hold the case for God to be almost a paradigm case of how one reasons *outside* the context of formal scientific method to an interesting and significant conclusion. Thus, my modest reflections will serve as an example of how one applies *interpretive* reasoning to the world and how this differs from one common (and I believe oversimplified) picture of *scientific* reasoning.

II

I will begin with a well-known parable (from which this essay takes its title). Some decades ago and English philosopher named Anthony Flew published an essay on belief and justification in which he drew the following analogy: suppose two men were arguing over whether a clear spot in a jungle was being deliberately tended by a gardener. They decide to test the question by observing the clearing and seeing whether any gardener shows up to tend the flowers there. When no gardener turns up one man concludes that there is no gardener. However, the other disagrees and maintains there is a gardener but that the gardener is invisible. Accordingly they set up electric fences and other barriers to stop the invisible gardener from entering. At night they hear no screams of an electrocuted man and in the morning find no traces of the fence being disturbed, nor have bloodhounds posted around the clearing smelled any intruder. At this point one would expect the man who believes in the invisible gardener to surrender his hypothesis. However, he does not. The gardener, he now maintains, is not just invisible but intangible as well. Moreover, he has no smell and makes no sound! At this point his partner throws up his hands. What, he asks, is the difference between an invisible, intangible gardener who makes no sound and emits no odor and no gardener at all?[19]

For Flew, the application of the parable to religious beliefs is easy and obvious. Meaningful beliefs, he holds, are subject to some form of empirical testing. We must be able to say under what conditions we would *reject* our belief in an invisible gardener if this belief is to have any purchase on reality. Similarly, we ought to be able to say under what conditions we would reject belief in God yet this is precisely what religious believers *do not* do and are precluded by the supposed virtue of faith from ever doing: when faced with recalcitrant facts such as the suffering of children the believer in God's reality and goodness qualifies and rationalizes but does not *abandon* his belief.

Now another philosopher named R. M. Hare objected that Flew misunderstood the basic character of religious belief. Belief in the goodness of God is not a testable proposition like the belief that there is beer in the fridge. Rather, religious beliefs are more in the nature of what he terms *bliks* or tacit points of view.[20] Consider the case of

---

[19] Anthony Flew, "Theology and Falsification," in *New Essays in Philosophical Theology*, ed. Anthony Flew and Alasdair MacIntyre (London: SCM Press, 1955), 267-268.

[20] It sounds odd to say that belief in God is a 'viewpoint' for surely the believer in

a paranoid who thinks all university dons are evil. One could point out all sorts of kind university dons as counter evidence but of course the paranoid will simply interpret their kindness as cunning. Hare points out that the problem with the paranoid does not lie in his powers of observation, which may be as sounds as anyone's, but in the backdrop against which he interprets what he observes, his *blik* as it were.[21] Now anyone who drives a car has a 'viewpoint' about the basic stability of matter and the continuity of the universe; no one expects their car to suddenly fall to pieces or the road to instantaneously vanish into a void. Yet it is rather hard to specify what falsifying instances would challenge this belief; anyone whose car *did* fall apart would look for an underlying *reason* such as shoddy engineering or sabotage.[22]

God thinks there is an actual divine entity, not simply that the world can be looked at *as if* it were a divine creation. Certainly, Flew objects that Hare is here being quite unorthodox and that religious believers are making clear assertions about what is the case. However, I think Hare's position can be adjusted to take this criticism into account. The view that 'God is good' is a proposition of the same sort as 'the earth revolves' or 'the sun is hot' and strikes me, as it does Hare, as simply wrong. Where Hare may mislead is in creating the unnecessary impression that belief in God is a 'viewpoint' in a purely subjective sense and no more. Perhaps I can illustrate. All we observe and all we can ever observe directly are physical impressions and thoughts. We have no way at all of verifying observationally that these impressions correspond to a world of people and things external to ourselves. For this reason the statement 'there are other minds' or 'there is an external world' is not like the statement 'dinner is in the oven'. However, we adopt as a viewpoint the belief that other minds and external objects exist and we are perfectly justified in doing so. In other words, we posit these entities on the basis of our interpretive stance and come to believe in those entities as our interpretive stance progressively and pragmatically justifies itself (in this case pretty quickly for there is no way one can go wrong believing in other minds). In this particular instance, I suspect our stance concerning other minds is a relational and ethical one primarily and an epistemic one (at first) only secondarily. The attitude or feeling that the universe is trustworthy translates reflectively into the proposition 'God exists' so that if this interpretive stance works for us we come to hold that God does indeed have some trans-subjective reality. Thus, on Hare's view a careful and qualified realism is still possible and the charge that he has replaced ordinary religious discourse with a fundamentally heterodox substitute can be answered.

[21] R. M. Hare, "Response to Anthony Flew," in *New Essays in Philosophical Theology*, ed. Anthony Flew and Alasdair MacIntyre (London: SCM Press, 1955), 268-269.

[22] In an important sense there is *no* verification of our belief in the uniformity of nature or indeed of the generality of *any* scientific theory for uniformity and generality concern predictions about what will happen in the future whereas observation concerns only the now. Strictly speaking, verification can occur nowhere but in the immediate present and it was to address this problem (the so-called problem of induction) that the notion of falsification was introduced. It is precisely the 'law-like' universality that makes a proposition scientific which is incapable of ver-

For Hare, a belief in God is more like our belief in the stability of matter and less like our belief that there is beer in the fridge so that questions of verification and falsification do not so clearly apply: the more fundamental and basic a belief is the less it is (or even can be) determined by data!

Now I cannot address here all the problems Flew and Hare have raised nor address all the responses this now-canonical exchange has generated. Suffice it to say that I think both have expressed valid intuitions. I think Hare is absolutely correct to point out that the concept of falsification Flew employs is far too crude: there is no way at all to specify what will count as a falsifying instance in a non-relative, context free manner. Absolutely speaking, there is no such thing as the verification or falsification of *any* proposition taken singly. One cannot refute materialism by pointing to a picture of a ghost or refute Atheism by pointing to the shroud of Turin: such phenomena can only persuade someone whose tacit assumptions about the world make the existence of ghosts or miraculous shrouds seem antecedently probable. Confirming or refuting instances only tell in the context of a person's total web of beliefs, values and commitments and hardly ever impinge at a single specifiable point. It is, as Hare puts it, a person's overall world-picture that determines which facts he regards as significant, how he interprets or understands those facts and indeed which facts he even notices. In a sense, there is no such thing as a 'fact' taken apart from our implicit or explicit theoretical constructions of the world. It is sensation *and* our background assumptions *together* that constitute meaningful perception. As the latter are multiple and open to reinterpretation on a number of levels we always have a choice as to how to revise our beliefs when confronted with an anomalous observation. To stick to our present example, the evils of the world always offer the theist a range of options: to abandon her belief in a

---

ification! As Imre Lakatos points out "One can today easily demonstrate that there can be no valid derivation of a law of nature from any finite number of facts; but we still keep reading about scientific theories being proved from facts" (*Science and Pseudo-Science*, 1) If it was in principle impossible to confirm a hypothesis because the process of verification extended indefinitely into the future it seemed more promising to say a theory could be falsified for falsifying observations need only occur in the present. However, for the reasons I indicate the falsification principle proves notoriously difficult to apply. (See Karl R. Popper, *Conjectures and Refutations: The Growth of Scientific Knowledge.* (New York: Harper & Row, 1968)). A thorough overview of the problem of induction and the various efforts to solve it can be found in "The Problem of Induction" by Wesley Salmon (*Philosophical Studies* vol.33 no. 1, 1978).

wise and loving creator or to revise one or several of her background concepts about the nature of wisdom and love. This holds in science as well. As W. V. O. Quine pointed out, it is only at its fringes that a scientific theory impinges on empirical facts: its core is protected from falsification by a ring of auxiliary hypotheses any of which can be sacrificed to save the underlying theory.[23] Thus, there is no such thing as a pure empirical refutation or confirmation of any core belief and this holds for science as much as it does for religion.

Now Flew is quite right to feel uncomfortable about this. If science operates the way Quine and others say it does then how can we distinguish it from the hermetic and self-enclosed world of the paranoid or conspiracy theorist who can fit any evidence whatever into their conceptual schemes? If viewpoints determine what facts we regard as significant and even what facts we notice how do we avoid relativism and skepticism? How do we determine which viewpoints we ought to adopt or whether we should alter the one we already have? This would be a difficult question to answer for a hard-core positivist but of course we are not in such a case for people adopt new points of view or change their point of view all the time. Indeed, in many cases they do so responsibly and intelligently. This is because there is much more to the process of justifying our points of view than a mechanical (and in practice quite ineffectual) process of experimental verification. Scientists and other thinkers and investigators are not just matching theories with data sets in a robotic and impersonal manner. As *persons* they possess values: moral and metaphysical beliefs, theological or political conceptions, aesthetic standards etc. all encoded within the practice of the knowledge community to which they belong. These values are crucial in determining how in a particular case data and theory are to interact.[24] Thus, anyone confronted with the evidence of the fossil

---

[23]W. V. O. Quine, "Two Dogmas of Empiricism," in *From a Logical Point of View* (Harvard University Press, 1961), Section 6, http://www.ditext.com/quine/quine.html The basic problem is this: if an observation falsifies a set of premises then either a. the fundamental theory is false b. some auxiliary hypotheses is false or c. some stated initial condition is false. However, no formalization of scientific method can say which of these three conditions obtains in a given instance leaving the scientist to muddle it out, perhaps abandoning his theory, perhaps modifying an auxiliary hypothesis etc. He is, however, never forced by observation to do the former rather than the *latter*.

[24]Helen Longino, writing in the context of feminist theory, makes this point well: "As a consequence of underdetennination, evidential relations must be understood as constituted by background assumptions which assert relations between the sorts of processes purportedly referred to by theoretical claims and the sorts of phenomena that serve as evidence for them. It follows that a suitable change in background

record could accept that the earth was at least many millions of years old. Alternatively, they could accept that God fabricated all of it 6000 years ago as a test of our faith. Empirically there is no difference at all between these two points of view. However, few would accept the latter as a serious alternative hypothesis because many people do not believe the existence of God is antecedently probable and many people who do believe in God fervently would not be inclined to attribute such deceit or arbitrariness to him. In this case, a theological assumption about either the existence or nature of God sharply limits the range of theories that can account for this particular data. Yet as this kind of assumption can often be only tacit, far in the back of one's mind as it were, it *looks* as if our current theory of the earth's age is being simply and directly read off from the facts.[25]

Of course many of these background assumptions are of a historical and contingent character. Some can even be rooted in class, racial or gender prejudice. Still, there is at least an argument to be made that certain values reflect an innate disposition of the mind. Complexity is not a good thing in a theory and is accepted only if the alternative is a theory that fits the facts poorly. Empirical accuracy is desirable but a less accurate theory might be preferred if it is simpler or coheres better with existing theories. Coherence is desirable but a more co-herent theory that was less than fruitful might not be. What we seek from a theory is some ideal (and almost never fully attained!) balance of unity, accuracy and productivity. These three ideals together con-stitute, as it were, the holy trinity of science and seem to be a kind of *conatus* or inborn *telos* of the mind. They are what allow us to judge between scientific theories as between overall world views in spite of the fact that raw empirical data can underwrite any number of alter-native theoretical formulations. Theories may compete with theories not facts but this competition need not be a blind or arbitrary one. Now the crucial thing to notice is that this judging between theories is an act of intelligence but *not* of methodical or formalized intelli-gence. There are no hard and fast rules to tell you how well a theory

assumption produces a change in evidential status." (Feminism and Philosophy of Science". 2)

[25]Perhaps one way to put this is by saying that we never simply see *that* without in some way seeing *as*. It may seem like a simple empirical proposition to say I see the planet Jupiter. However 'planet' is a theoretical construct: if, in some *Solaris* like scenario, Jupiter turned out to be sentient then, of course, I have never seen the 'planet' Jupiter at all. There is, of course, the patch of light that all of us can see but this bit of sense data is an *abstraction* from the object of perception, not the object itself.

should fit the data or when it has gotten too complex and encumbered with *ad hoc* hypotheses. Decisions between theories are acts of interpretive judgment proceeding in a personal yet nonetheless responsible manner. *Even in science itself*, there is a function of intelligence that does not proceed by formal induction or deduction or by experimental verification or falsification but by free pragmatic decision or, to use Aristotle's term, *phronesis* or 'prudence'.

Science, then, is a special subset of hermeneutic or interpretive reason applied to physical nature (to natural signs as opposed to abstract symbols). Theology is a special subset of hermeneutic or interpretive reason applied to the sacred texts, creeds and faith practices of a religious community. Literary criticism is a special subset of interpretive reason applied to poems, plays and novels. Interpretive reason functions in science in a crucial way but can function just as well *outside* of science in areas where formalized methods of induction, say, cannot realistically be applied. Hermeneutic judgment and the virtues that underlie it are the bond that unites our theoretical constructions with the given of the empirical world. I believe such judgment can be employed intelligently on the question of God's existence and in the next section of this essay I will try to show how this might be done. My effort may convince nobody; certainly, there will be nothing in it to compel anyone's assent. This does not bother me in the least. It is sometimes intimated that the problem with interpretive reasoning is that it fails to produce conclusive results. While science *answers* questions, philosophy, classics and history simply *discuss* them to no ultimate conclusion. Thus, while science can throw Ptolemy in the trash philosophers are still talking about Thales. I think this criticism is misplaced for 'results' are never so certain as people take them for and are quite over-rated anyway. Aristotle once said that it is as foolish to expect mathematical demonstration from the student of ethics as it is to expect rhetoric from a geometer. One can expect no more certainty and precision than a subject allows. Most of the things discussed in the humanities allow for knowledge on the level of well-considered opinion. It is not the conclusiveness of answers that makes humanities valuable but the importance of the questions it addresses. Thinking one had 'results' concerning these fundamental questions would show a real ignorance of their nature: to borrow a distinction from Gabriel Marcel, love, evil, death, goodness, freedom etc. are not 'problems' to be solved but 'mysteries' to be lived and contemplated.[26] The following, then, is my considered opinion on the question of God. There may well be some higher level of certainty possible here but I make no claim to possess it nor do I think I need to make such a claim to establish the basic thesis of this book.

III

What then of the question with which we began? Is the hypothesis of a God like the invisible gardener an object of blind belief that relates itself to no evidence and whose existence can be falsified by no observation of fact? Where in the garden might we look for his presence if this is at all detectable? I have already given my opinion that the existence of God is not an empirical question if by this one means that one can specify which observations or conditions would obtain if God existed and which would not. For one thing, if by God one means 'creator of heaven and earth' then of course God is the ultimate condition of any and all observable facts, the world as a totality being the evidence for his reality. For Flew this would render the concept of God un-falsifiable and hence meaningless. How does one test a hypothesis that predicts anything and everything? The best one could do might be to form the (shaky) surmise that a universe created by God would contain less evil and suffering than ours. In this case the existence of God would at least appear to be highly unlikely. However, I do not think that that observation by itself is the only way to form an intelligent judgment. I have given several examples above of disciplines in which we make judgments about objects without resorting to the methods of the physical sciences. Among these disciplines is one in which we ask (and haltingly attempt to answer) certain kinds of global questions about the whole or totality of which we are a part: I refer, of course, to the discipline of philosophy. If an Atheist or sceptic is asked his opinion on life after death he or she may well respond that consciousness and personality, like all things, depends on the physical substrate of the universe so that immortality is impossible in a non-physical form and difficult to countenance in a physical form. This

---

[26]I should point out that by 'mystery' Marcel does *not* mean something unintelligible. A mystery is a phenomenon like evil or love in which the subject is necessarily implicated: a mystery is as fundamental and inexhaustible as we are to ourselves. In contrast, a 'problem', such as an algebraic equation, is something from which we 'remove' ourselves in quest of a determinate solution. Thus, the contemplation of a mystery is a moment in reflexive or self-knowledge as opposed to object knowledge. (Gabriel Marcel, *Being and Having*, trans. Katharine Farrer (Westminster: Dacre Press, 1949), 185-187).

is a philosophical opinion because it is pointing not to some specific, contingent fact but to an underlying condition of any and all facts: everything there is must be material. While a scientist might say that a particular kind of matter (like water) boils at a certain temperature a philosopher might point to matter as a comprehensive principle unifying all those phenomena that we call natural. Conversely, if one agrees with Aristotle one will hold that an underlying condition of the goal-directed behavior of animals is the pure actuality of God the unmoved mover. These are philosophical positions because they concern not facts and their generalization into laws but comprehensive or boundary conditions of the kinds of facts we observe: positivism itself tries to state a comprehensive or boundary condition of meaningful discourse, leaving it with the intractable problem of how, as a theory, it can meet its own criterion of meaningfulness!

With this in mind let us now return to Flew's garden. There is no particular fact about this garden that tells conclusively for or against the presence of an invisible gardener. Given that the gardener is invisible and leaves no tangible trace of his presence it does not appear that there *can* be any such facts. So, Flew asks, what is the difference between such a gardener and no gardener at all? This question is legitimate but there are many ways of trying to answer it. Rather than looking for confirming or disconfirming instances of our invisible gardener hypothesis we might ask a different question: are there global features of the garden as a whole that could be taken as traces or signs of a gardener? If we look at our universe as a whole or look globally at some part or aspect of it can we find traces or signs that point to a God? I think in fact that we can. Moreover, I think these sign of divine presence are (for me) of sufficient strength to counterbalance any of the corresponding signs of divine absence (though anyone is free to come to the opposite conclusion). In short, though God's presence cannot be tested for it can be responsibly *read from* the text of the world.

Let us consider some of the conclusions we reached in part II of this essay. We saw that if we look at the phenomena of science as a totality its success seems to depend upon some fundamental features of the mind and its operations. Specifically, we saw that science, like all intelligent inquiry has a tripartite structure or character. It is concerned with facts but not simply with facts. It is concerned with theories but not simply with theories. Far from being value-neutral it has basic moral, intellectual and aesthetic values built into it yet the values of science have to be embodied in theoretical formulations grounded in empirical data. Science is thus concerned with coordinating the empirically-given with some theoretical framework or structure in the best way possible. In short, science is concerned with being, intelligible order and goodness. In good science these three work together as a kind of unity to give us a glimpse into the truth. If I take any of these elements in abstraction or separation from the others I find it crumbles in my hand. Remove values from science and theories can never be matched to data. Remove theory and facts are simply mute. Remove data and theory is an empty self-enclosed abstraction (data being the contingent or materially-individuated moment in the unfolding of knowledge). What is more, science is this way because the mind is this way: it seeks the unity and coherence of the real in an economic and aesthetically-satisfying way. If then, we step back from some particular application of the mind to look at some of its more general, global features we find that it involves a basic drive towards the integration of three things that are distinct but nonetheless mutually imply each other.

Of course one can just leave it at that and draw no further conclusions but I am struck by a further fact: every specific instance of our attempts to co-ordinate being, intelligibility and goodness is some sort of failure. Fact is fudged to fit the coherence of a theory. Simplicity is compromised when *ad hoc* hypotheses are used to adjust for empirical anomalies. The implicit values of scientists cause them to violate basic intellectual principles of coherence and accuracy because they turn out, on examination, to be rooted in prejudice or self-interest. Scientific theories can be in many respects lousy but, like democracy, are the worst theories except for all the others. In other words, anything *we* can construct is a kind of rough approximation of our tripartite ideal. Yet at the same time we know that this is a problem with us and our limitations rather than a problem with the ideal as such. It is odd to find at the root of one's thinking an ideal that is as hard and objective as any fact yet is nowhere truly exemplified in the world. One might just shrug one's shoulders at this of course; nothing necessitates taking this reflection any further. Yet the mind's spontaneity is to move from one thing to the next so I will let my thoughts flow onwards and see what results.

One thought that forms in my mind not as a necessary inference perhaps but as a natural concomitant is that the reason I cannot separate goodness, intelligibility and reality in my mind is that they are inseparable in reality. In reality they are one thing expressed in three modes and I discover this negatively every time I try to hive off one from the other and treat it as if it were the whole. Yet as I look out on the world I do not in fact find this co-inherence expressed anywhere with full adequacy. Things which seem in themselves, in their true nature, to be one are in this world multiple and divided. How to account for this need to affirm the unity of what seems to be nowhere one and whole seems puzzling: very puzzling unless I reverse my perspective and assume *not* that 'reality' is not some dim approximation of a non-existent ideal but that the broken fragmented world I am looking at is a kind of approximation or image of a reality that is full and whole in itself. I arrive thus at the notion that what is in itself is one self-generating, self-sustaining substantial whole that nonetheless fully embraces difference or plurality within itself: I arrive, in fact, at the notion of God as the objective synthesis of all values. This is not a proof in any demonstrative sense: perhaps it could be developed into one but that is probably beyond my talents. In fact though, my preference is to leave it for now in this somewhat rough form for reasons I will state below. So, reader, you are free to reject any premise of this argument as you are free not to follow any of it to its natural but not inevitable conclusion. At best I have engaged in a sort of weak abduction or inference to a possible best explanation.

Still, I think my hypothesis a satisfactory one for my purposes. It explains for me both why I have the aspirations that I do (my mind is seeking the whole or totality that is objective in God) and why I consistently fail to achieve those aspirations (I am a finite creature divided within myself). What is more, I see that it has certain benefits: the notion of a transcendent principle that cannot be captured and defined in terms of our usual binaries prevents me from falling into one-sided or dogmatic thinking. I know there is an *Other* that puts all the fixity and rigidity of my determinations into question. Being open to that Other, this beyond I cannot quite grasp or reduce, allows me to be more open to the otherness that I encounter in the everyday world. Indeed, as there strikes me as something false and abstract about opposing the conceptually-ideal with the real (what is an ideal without reality?) I scarcely find I can think of this ideal in any other way than as supremely objective, its reality being a kind of outflow or emanation of its goodness and perfection. Thus does the spontaneous living movement of thought lead to a lively perception of the divine reality which *can* but need not be submitted to as real, this last step being an assent of the will beyond the necessity of intellect though grounded in its natural operation. With this assent comes a life and practice grounded in it and this, taken as a kind of whole, provides all the 'verification' or 'falsification' my hypothesis needs. To date, I find that this notion of a transcendent other has spared me many of the missteps of reductive, deterministic or one-sided thinking so that I have come progressively to confirm experientially my original intuition that in the idea of perfection I have grasped an underlying principle of order: the notion has yet to fail me in any crucial thing so I take it as more or less confirmed. Moreover it seems to mesh well with a host of other phenomena: the experiential testimony of mystics, the charity of the saints, intimations of the sacred in the beauty of nature or in the mystery of personhood as it reveals itself to us in love and ethical responsibility. Though any part of this chain of reasons and motivations can be rejected or doubted, together they add up to a sufficiently solid presentation to move my will to a free assent. However, that is an exercise of judgment on my part that a particular stance is well justified; it imposes no necessity on anyone else any more than a sound reading of *King Lear* precludes another differing one.

My more skeptical readers may well be thinking that I say all this only by way of justifying something I believed in beforehand. They are absolutely right about this: I follow this little chain of discursive considerations to the conclusion I do because I happen to be the person I am. There may indeed be some underlying human need or basic sentiment that forms the backdrop to our notions of God. Whether one describes this as a 'feeling of absolute dependence', an 'awe at the given', a 'longing for wholeness', a 'sense of the providential' or what have you is not important for my present purpose: the beginning of *my* search must have involved some inchoate but partially thematic *idea* of the thing I was looking for. No doubt, this was provided for me by the family and culture I was raised in, my early experiences, books I read, art works that moved me, etc. All of these things no doubt predisposed me to push my reflections in the direction I did until I arrived at the thing I was seeking. To all of the above I plead guilty and offer in my defense the fact that I am human. As Plato would have it, philosophy begins with opinion and your opinions come from the world you grow up in and the influences to which you are exposed. Indeed, it does not seem too much to say that a kind of faith, or pre-reflective tending and receptivity of the mind to signs of divine presence underwrites any rational ascent to God, as was admitted by Augustine and Anselm among many others. This faith may be a matter of the heart in some sense but even so it is elicited by external mediations as well and so retains an (apparent) element of historical contingency.

It may disappoint and dismay many of my readers to hear this, but I have come to think of the openness and contingency in which these reflections are embedded to be their strength rather than their weakness. Indeed, I tend to think a stronger argument than I have offered here would have certain disadvantages. As I said above, it is not the discursive intellect that is converted but the person as a whole: intellect does not move apart from will. If secular humanism has one crucial moral insight it is that the notion of God or Gods as external agents to whom we must bow is one that slights our freedom and dignity. A rationalistic God to whom we bowed only out of logical necessity would simply be an external fact. As Sartre pointed out, such a God would be incompatible with my freedom, something merely *imposed* on me like gravity. But God, as the highest freedom, can only truly be encountered personally, as the beyond in and through which we encounter others. Thus, the ascent to God as I have tried to lay it out here is an unconstrained movement from the inner core of the person that has traces and signs aplenty to reach its goal should it desire to look but is under no compulsion to do so: anything more or less than this would conclude not to God, but to an idol on which all the wrath of Atheists would justly fall.

So, I have not established the existence of God if by that one means that I have run over Atheists and Agnostics with an intellectual bull-dozer. This is to over-rate what discursive reason can do and indeed to confirm it in one of its characteristic vices: the notion that the search for truth is a contest which one wins by battering one's opponents with arguments instead of clubs. What I do think I have shown is that a *theistic* interpretation of the mind and its operations is possible, indeed natural and plausible. What is more, I have indicated that, as an interpretive stance, the theistic stance is one that in my experience has tended to confirm itself pragmatically over time so that, for me, it has taken on the status of a 'verified' hypothesis. I have come to this conclusion *not* by any formalized procedure of deduction, induction or experimental verification but by an exercise of judgment which has attained not certainty but the firmness of (personal) conviction appropriate to an exercise of interpretive reasoning. In this I believe I have exercised my mind responsibly though I may *not* have compelled any neutral third party observer to adopt my hypothesis. The reader who is dissatisfied with this can find many authors, both secular and religious, who make more ambitious claims and offer more bracing certainties. He or she is welcome to peruse their books if this one disappoints.

4 DAWKINS AND THEOLOGY

I

Mr. Richard Dawkins is no fan of theology; so much so that he has written 500 pages on God without making any serious reference to it. One searches his bibliography in vain for references to Rahner, Lonergan, Pannenberg, Moltmann, Von Balthassar, or Barth. Liberation and feminist theology do not exist. Nor do such up-to-the-minute figures as Jean Luc Marion or John Milbank. Of course, his critics, such as Terry Eagleton and John Cornwell, have not been slow to point this out: how, they ask, can Dawkins write a book about God that ignores all that the brightest and best have had to say and still be taken seriously?[27] On what other subject would a man be permitted such willful ignorance? However Dawkins will not be shamed on this account. He knows nothing about theology and refuses on principle to know anything about it. Why, he asks, should he bother studying something whose basic premise he rejects? He has, after all, demonstrated that God's existence is astronomically improbable. Is it not plain as day that all theology is thus rendered useless at a stroke so that it would be a sad waste of anyone's time to examine it? Indeed, in the preface to the paperback edition of *The God Delusion* Dawkins offers us the following analogy: does the boy in Grimm's tale need to know the scholarly literature on invisible garments before he can say the emperor has no clothes? Does he need to con the state of learned opinion on fairies and leprechauns before disbelieving in them? It is clear that Dawkins believes this retort a masterstroke of subtlety. His

---

[27]Eagleton has attacked Dawkins in an article entitled "Lunging Flailing and Mis-punching" published in the *London Review of Books* 28, no. 20 (2006): 32-34. Cornwell's critique is contained in *Darwin's Angel: An Angelic Riposte to* The God Delusion (London: Profile Books, 2007).

acolytes seem to agree for they repeat it *ad nauseam* whenever the charge of anti-intellectualism is brought forth.

On one level, of course, it is an inept response. I do not at all *believe* in astrology but I would hardly assert on that basis that I could quickly and easily demonstrate its falsity without reading a single book on the subject. There are two clear senses in which Dawkins is responsible for knowing some theology and to that extent the complaints of Eagleton and Cornwell appear to me justified. Firstly, as the so called *natural* theology offers arguments and evidence for a conclusion opposed to his own Dawkins should have at least some basic grasp of the rudiments of this tradition. For instance, he should minimally know Aquinas' five ways from the primary text and not repeat garbled versions of them he has found on the web. Indeed, his discussions (such as they are) of figures like Anselm, Pascal and Kant make it painfully obvious that he has only read a very little *about* their arguments and has not engaged their texts at all. Dawkins' discussion of natural theology, thus, does not meet even the minimal standards of intellectual probity one would expect in a popular work.[28] Secondly, as Dawkins has a fair bit to say about the Bible he is responsible for knowing something (anything!) about what is called *revealed* theology or the branch of theology that concerns what is (putatively) known of God from scripture. Here he has not made even fumbling efforts for his reading of the Bible is completely innocent of *any* interpretive tradition: Jewish, Christian or even secular.

However, I suspect there is a larger issue here than one man's laziness, obstinate stupidity or *hubris*. I have said some harsh things so far but the purpose of this book is not polemic. Dawkins and his devotees are, in any case, implacably forearmed against any and every criticism of the kind I have enunciated. Thus, continuing in a polemical vein

---

[28] As a reader with some philosophical training I find myself in an awkward position. I do not want to pile on to Dawkins yet his discussion of the traditional proofs of the existence of God, which he seems to regard as definitive, impresses only for its astounding puerility. Much of it is in fact simple mockery without the barest attempt at analysis. Moreover, he misstates just about every argument he touches on, often dropping key premises. If the reader thinks this judgment harsh she may consult any number of books by Thomists, Process Philosophers, Idealists or others interested in natural theology and make the comparison herself. I could name dozens of books here but one I happen to admire is *Atheism and Theism* by Errol E. Harris. One of the things that always brings me up short with Dawkins is that he is asking his readers to literally believe that whole libraries full of books contain millions of words of gibberish, books which on his own admission he has not so much as glanced at.

would be a waste of time. I believe the reason for this is fundamental: Dawkins has an epistemology and metaphysics radically at odds with humanistic critics such as Eagleton and Cornwell. In fact, he has an epistemology and metaphysics radically at odds with the humanities itself. To state this briefly, for Dawkins, being is fact and knowledge is taking a look (for Dawkins on truth see below). Thus, the study of Aquinas is unnecessary for his arguments; if they mean anything at all, mean nothing more and nothing less than what they appear to at first glance: so much so that a bald summary of them is no different in principle from the primary text. The Bible too is understood once the literal meaning of the sentences that compose it is grasped. This is the ontology and epistemology of Puritan plain speaking. What Dawkins seems to oppose is what I would label *the metaphysics of interpretation* and the culture of secondary discourse founded on it: the view that being is in some sense text or sign and that knowing is not a matter of looking at what is there but the terminus of a process of criticism and dialogue: in short, Dawkins views knowing as *seeing* where 'humanists' view knowing as *reading.* Thus, he will engage in no learned disquisitions with Thomistic scholarship or biblical hermeneutics: these belong to secondary traditions of commentary that muddy the plain sense of the original which, unless it is arrant nonsense, should be directly graspable by the proverbial man on the street.

That Dawkins' distaste for interpretive traditions is grounded historically in certain radical expressions of fundamentalist religiosity seems obvious. It explains his persistent tendency to assume, even when challenged, that fundamentalist religion is religion simply. It matters little to Dawkins that the confessions of millions of Catholic, Orthodox, Anglican, Mainline Protestant and Evangelical believers commit them to nothing resembling scriptural literalism: belief in *Genesis* is belief in a six-day creation and a literal flood. Dawkins, of course, claims that this is merely a descriptive judgment. Religion as he describes it in *The God Delusion* is religion as *ordinary people* believe it. Not that he has the faintest curiosity about what or how ordinary people believe: Dawkins' treatment of religion is as innocent of sociology as it is of any other humane discipline. Large numbers of Americans may *say* they believe in a six day creation but of course the real question is what they *mean* by saying this. It is difficult to believe that for the majority of them it is an expression of abstract theological principle: in many cases it is surely a marker of social, political and regional identity. People turn to religion for all kinds of reasons (affective and practical) and there is little ground for thinking their primary interest is in biblical interpretation, literal or otherwise.[29] As it would be no great task for Dawkins to discover this his tendency to equate religion with fundamentalist literalism must surely be taken as a *normative* judgment: it is the Pat Robertsons of the world who represent 'real' religion because it is they, rather than the 'sophisticated theologians', who share his metaphysic of being as fact and his epistemology of knowing as taking a look. Thus, they are the only ones who appear to him to be saying something of relevance to the question of God for it is only they who seem to be asserting literal facts.

Now my intention in this essay is not to convince Dawkins to start plowing through the heavy German authors listed above. For one thing, it would do a man of his background and interests precious little good. The metaphysics of text is a way of looking at things every bit as much as the metaphysics of fact: if someone adopts the second stance no amount of hectoring or ridicule will cause her to adopt the first. If your grumpy old uncle insists that Schoenberg is noise and that Jackson Pollock is random splatters of paint there is no tribunal you can appeal to that will show him wrong. All you can do is invite him to take a second listen or a second look and hope that his looking becomes understanding and his listening appreciation. The following essay is an invitation to consider religion from the standpoint of being as text and knowledge as interpretation; from this standpoint it does not and indeed cannot appear as the idiotic delusion Secular Humanists assert that it is. In short, if we start from the primacy not of empirical fact but from the primacy of symbol religion becomes a rich field of

---

[29]Indeed the most cursory examination of history reveals that far from being the natural stance of *homo religiosis* fundamentalist beliefs have been inculcated by theological authority in conscious reaction to the liberal theologies of the 19th century. It is a certain *theological community* that has insisted on literal inerrancy in the scriptures and not the ordinary person in the pews. In fact, in a manner contemporary readers will find familiar, the founding of the fundamentalist movement in 1909 was crucially aided by the brothers Lyman and Milton Stewart who put up the funds for the publication of the first fundamentalist tracts. (Cole, 52-53) Dawkins' account of fundamentalism is thus precisely opposite to what the evidence indicates, surely an awkward situation for so die-hard an empiricist. At any rate many even in the Evangelical wing of Christianity have moved on from the kind of literalism Dawkins seems to think is universally normative (Livingston and Fiorenza, 406-7). A better account of the actual spirit of contemporary Christianity, which is on the whole ethical and affective rather than doctrinal and confessional, is given by Graeme Smith *A Short History of Secularism* (see 4, 67-88).

study rather than a tissue of error and folly. This is an important advantage: if the metaphysics of interpretation can make richer sense of central human phenomena like religion than its rivals then this is a serious point in its favor for it is thereby shown to have greater comprehensiveness and scope. I believe I can show that it does so in the second and third parts of this essay. In particular, I hope to show that the dichotomy between the images and narratives of 'popular' religion and the conceptualizations of philosophers and theologians is only relative: both belong to differing but complementary moments of the phenomenon of religion.[30]

II

In Ursula Le Guin's science fiction novel *The Dispossessed* there is a character from an austere desert moon who visits a lush, prosperous planet where he takes in, for the first time in his life, a movie. What puzzles and annoys him most about it is that the comedy of the film rests on a long string of double entendres. Why, he asks, do people talk about sex by *not* talking about sex? Why, the first year student of poetry asks, does Keats not *say what he means directly* about beauty and mortality rather than going on about urns and nightingales? Why, the rationalist might snort, would the bible communicate by symbols and metaphors? If God had something to say to the human race would he not just say it directly and have done? Why have this displaced mode of discourse instead of uttering propositions that say directly what they mean and correspond directly to facts in the world? Why can't language be a glassy mirror in which we can see all things clearly reflected back to us? Why should the bible be written in an intricate code that depends on scholars or other adepts to interpret? Should God not speak directly and simply to every human being? I suspect these sorts of questions lie behind much of the resistance to a hermeneutic and interpretive approach to religion and indeed to the world. Symbol and poetry seem to give us over to the private, subjective and esoteric: after all, to whom or what is one responsible when reading symbols? If text is unmoored from fact what governs

---

[30]Even among academic students of religion there is sometimes a strange reluctance to regard 'intellectual' religion as 'real' religion, as if the philosophy of Maimonides or the poetry of Blake is somehow not a religious phenomenon. I take it as a given that an intellectual or artist who is religious will put her faculties of intellect or creativity at the service of her religious ideals exactly as another person might use their hands or feet. It is a strange (perhaps Christian?) bias that associates religion with simplicity and simplicity with absence of thought.

its interpretation? Is the reading of symbols not arbitrary? If text is metaphor is its meaning not at the whim of the priestly interpreter whether that priest be a cleric or secular academic? If so, the culture of interpretation would sort poorly with the secular liberal belief that democracy and freedom depend on a realm of publically accessible, certifiable facts.

This essay cannot answer all these concerns comprehensively. My more modest goal is to suggest that there is a deep underlying necessity to symbolic discourse so that religion can appear (at first) in no other way than as metaphor, myth and image. I also want to show that this is in no way to the detriment of religion for myth and image are indispensible ways of knowing. At the same time I do not want to romanticize the mythic as the pure, pristine original mode of apprehension tainted by the murderous blight of analytic thought. If myth in its original form is a narrative construction of reality constituted by performance and ritual the significance of most myths for us is as read, interpreted and understood. We are, for the most part, in a self-conscious relation to the mythic dimension (at least as experienced by ancient and non-Western cultures) where we attempt to derive explicit meanings from them, whether these be theological, philosophical or psychological (in the manner say of Freud and Jung). This reflective differentiation of the primary totality of myth is part and parcel of our freedom; we can assess and appropriate the myths of the Greeks or Vikings because we are not bound to them. Our stance is one of interpretation rather than direct participation. So, another aspect of my argument will be that, for good or ill, the primacy of symbol means for us a culture of reading and its attendant metaphysics: we will have such beasts as critics, scholars and even (alas!) theologians who give us their considered view about *what all these things mean.*

So, why symbols rather than plain sense? One possible answer is given by Thomas Aquinas. I do not know if it stands as a final answer but it at least seems to me a good place to begin. In his *Summa of Theology* (Question 1, Article 9) Aquinas considers the exact question I have raised here. Why, he asks, should "Holy Scripture use metaphors?". There seem to be three reasons why it should not. Firstly "... to proceed by the aid of various similitudes and figures is proper to poetry, the least of all the sciences". Secondly, sacred doctrine is intended "... to make truth clear... but by such similitudes truth is obscured, therefore to put forward divine truths under the likeness of corporeal things does not befit this doctrine". Thirdly, the "...higher creatures are, the nearer they approach to the divine likeness. If, therefore, any creature be taken to represent God, this representation ought chiefly to be taken from higher creatures, and not from lower...". However, Aquinas holds that "God provides for everything according to the capacity of its nature. Now it is natural to man to attain to intellectual truths through sensible things, because all our knowledge originates from sense. Hence, in holy scripture spiritual truths are fittingly taught under the likeness of material things". This is not problematic for him because "poetry makes use of metaphors to produce a representation, for it is natural to man to be pleased with representations". Also "the ray of divine revelation is not extinguished by the sensible imagery wherewith it is veiled" but these raise men "to the knowledge of intelligible truths". Moreover, representations of God taken from physical nature (rather than spiritual beings) have the advantage of being *so* obviously inappropriate that they cannot be mistaken for literal assertions: few, for instance, would really hold that God has arms though the bible represents him as such.

There is much to consider in this medieval doctrine but I want to focus on one aspect of it. Although all our clichés about medieval thought regard it as dualistic and anti-body in orientation the point of Aquinas' teaching is to underline the role of the body in human knowing. Our thinking occupies a mid-point between intellect and sense such that we can never grasp the abstract without some reference to the concrete (and vice versa). Indeed, even the most refined speculation (insofar as it is discursive) involves some measure of *thinking in images*. Thus, even the most abstract of concepts involve some suppressed metaphor. The notion of substance, for instance, involves the picture or image of something standing under or behind something else though one would be naïve to think that Aristotle *understood* substance in such grossly spatial terms. When we speak about mind and consciousness we often use the image of physical mirroring, as when we speak of reflecting on or about something. Of course, words like substance and reflection are no longer images for us for we have become so accustomed to their formal philosophical usage that we tend to forget the metaphors on which they are based. What Aquinas is saying above is that human beings have a special way of knowing that involves both body and mind at once so that thoughts exist in us as signs and symbols that unify sense and intellect. This, he claims, is why the Word of God comes to us in stories and images and not in pure propositions: this reflects *how we as bodily beings come to know* which is by rendering actually intelligible what is only potentially so, the images and representations of sense and imagination.

The broader insight I want to draw out from this medieval reflection can perhaps be stated like this: if we come to some kind of unity or wholeness *with* ourselves, some kind of actualization of our potential, it is out of some disruption, displacement or difference *from* ourselves. This sounds forbiddingly abstract but in fact it is a truth easy to illustrate. A poet who wishes to speak the truth about herself will as often as not (unless she is very gifted) utter a heap of prevarications and rationalizations if she attempts to do so directly: if she truly wants to reveal her being to others a much more effective way of doing so is to speak about something *other* than herself, even if this is only a crow sitting on a wire. Think too of how much more fully we come to inhabit our own bodies when its rhythms are externalized in music. Even a child comes to learn its place in the world through imagining itself as what it is not; as when the nature of its developing humanity is explored by pretending to be dogs or dinosaurs. Art, music and play all involve self-exploration through displacement into another, whether this other is words, images, sounds or objects of mimesis. In short, self-actualization is an activity of *self-expression* in and through another whereby we *image* what is within us and bring it to our conscious awareness. This self-actualization is accomplished most effectively in activities like art and sport which are intrinsically fulfilling and free of external compulsion. If you like, coming to self-knowledge is a process of self-imaging-in-delight in which a moment of struggle or effort in relation to something external leads to heightened awareness of self and world. The most basic and original form of this is mind itself, which comes into possession of its powers by 'intellectualizing' objects it encounters in perception through the medium of imaginative representation.

The mediating link in this process is (for thinkers like Aquinas and Aristotle) the activity of the imagination, which is poised, as it were, midway between thinking and sensing. The imaginative faculty constructs for us out of the dizzying variety of sensation a structured representation of the perceptual world. It is this representation that the intellect uses to develop its higher-order conceptualizations. If the picture I have been painting above is accurate, it will come as no surprise whatsoever if universal truths of experience are expressed first in stories and pictures, if *image,* not the late abstraction of *fact,* is the first mode in which we think. In this respect it is perhaps striking that we meet our earliest ancestors today primarily through their marvelous cave-paintings. Thus, it is *not* the case that we can hypothesize some early human, an original literalist as it were, who possessed nothing but sense impressions out of which he proceeded to construct his world as one would erect a building out of bricks: narrative must lie already at the basis of knowing for it is narrative construction that first constitutes connected experience.[31] The drive to unity and connectivity that lies at the basis of speculative thought appears, as Aristotle informs us, in its first form in the stories of the poets.[32] Why? Because, he informs us, *mimesis* or imitation is natural to human beings. It is how they know and how they grow: we form a conception of the world around us by *representing* its form and action. Indeed, if we follow Swiss psychoanalyst Carl Jung, even the most basic, pre-conscious levels of the psyche contain symbolic representations of instincts and desires or so-called 'archetypes': as if the *image* was basic and essential to human life itself.[33]

Indeed, if we look back on how the archaic Greeks, the Hebrews, the Egyptians and the Babylonians conceived of the world we find that they did so in narrative terms: they told *stories* about how things were before there was any developed conception of a separate realm of 'facts' to which the stories did or did not correspond (for the Ancients the alternative to a story was another story, as in the Hebrew retelling of the Babylonian flood myth). The story-teller described the world, to be sure, but at the same time he constituted or generated the world so described: this is perhaps why so many stories of these ancient peo-

---

[31] Here I will cite some excellent observations by Northrop Frye: "...demotic habits of language have always been with us, and it would be easy to assume that poetry, however ancient, is still a later development out of an original demotic speech. It is very difficult for many twentieth-century minds to believe that poetry is genuinely primitive, and not an artificial way of decorating and distorting ordinary "prose"...But the point goes deeper than this. It is not only that the real meaning (of Psalm 19) is metaphorical and that any superstitious "literal" view of it would have seemed as absurd to the original writer as to us...the images are *radically* metaphorical: this is the only way in which language can convey the sense of the presence of a numinous personality in the world, and that is where we stop." Frye, *The Great Code* (Toronto: Academia Press, 1982) 24.

[32] *Metaphysics Alpha*, Ch. 3, 983-984.

[33] Jung says "The primordial image might be described as the instinct's perception of itself, or as the self portrait of the instinct." ("Instinct and the Unconscious" 56) Elsewhere he adds:" In Plato, however, an extra-ordinarily high value is set on the archetypes as metaphysical ideas, a paradigms or models, while real things are held only to be copies of these model ideas. Medieval philosophy from the time of St. Augustine-from whom I have borrowed the idea of the archetype- down to Malebranche and Bacon, still stands on a Platonic footing in this respect." (55)

ples dealt with creation, such as the Babylonian *Enuma Elish* or the Hebrew *Genesis*. *Poesis* is a form of *cosmogenesis*: it is not a clumsy attempt at factual description but a mode of knowing by making.[34] If what Aquinas (following Aristotle) says is true (and I think it is) our first awareness of the world will express itself in no other way than as imaginative representations: certainly it will not express itself in 'truth functional propositions' about 'atomic facts', 'raw feels' or any of the other beasts that philosophers have claimed are the primitive basis of human knowledge. These entities are constituted by a certain phase of reflective consciousness (subject/object duality) rather as gods, demons and ancestors are among the basic entities constituted by myth. In either case, we can see that knowing involves active construction by the imagination as well as passive registering of sense data.

Even today it remains true that poets are, as Shelley would have it, the unacknowledged legislators of the world. The reflective differentiations of analytic science operate only locally on physical fact: their overarching context is metaphorical and narrative. Thus, nature is a machine or a kingdom with laws, evolution a process of 'selection', D.N.A. a code, etc. These metaphors are not just flowery description; they are regulative and heuristic and science cannot be shorn of them. Thus, imaginative projection still plays a role in the constitution of science and though the scientist may seek to 'demythologize' this or that phenomenon he does so within a deeper standpoint that remains in essence symbolic: science as much as poetry remains an exercise in representative thinking. This is no doubt why a culture's politics so frequently anticipates its science. Thus, the social models of Hellenistic Greece underlie the atomism of Epicurus as the politics of Burke suggests the nature of Darwin. Our failure to recognize this fact lies perhaps in the worry that this somehow de-legitimates the sci-

---

[34]The difference between mythic and scientific conceptions of the world is that for *mythos* being (unless otherwise indicated) is assumed to be active self-generating spontaneity and so the world is described through the model of a great society, or macrocosm, in which the stories of gods and heroes transpire. Reality, for this standpoint, is fundamentally narrative. For modern science (leaving aside the question of post-modern science) being is assumed (unless otherwise indicated) to be inert passivity described through the model of a machine whose parts are externally related. The world, fundamentally, is objectivity. I would hope by now the reader has given up the totalizing perspective which worries about which of these models is absolutely true (as opposed to which is most fruitful in a given context) and has noted the fundamental affinity between them: they are two great foundational metaphors of our civilization.

entific enterprise, which, according to one ideology of science, differs
from poetry or religion in being rigorously quantitative and 'objec-
tively factual', i.e, read *from* the world in a detached, impersonal way
rather than read *into* it. One casualty of the assault of scientific positivism on metaphor and interpretive reasoning is science itself as soon
as these are seen to be constitutive of it. Suffice it to say that while
the perspective I am taking here does undermine one way of justifying
the hegemony of science over all other discourses it leaves science as
an activity, craft or humane interest perfectly intact.

We can now see, hopefully, that religion, science and art have a
common grounding in the representative imagination and are essentially symbolic products and that this is of no detriment to either of
them. Of course, for reflective intelligence, there is no paradise of
the primary: discursive rationality is aware of the distinction of the
representation and the thing represented. Thus, we have art critics
who expound for us the neo-platonic conceptions of Michelangelo and
Botticelli. We have literary critics who explain to us the politics of
Shakespeare or the religion of Blake. We have interpreters of scripture and theologians who codify religious experience as doctrine. In
the last century or so we have had philosophers of science: realists,
constructivists and instrumentalists who try to tell us what science is
and what status we should attribute to the entities it posits. In short,
any primary projection is potentially an object of secondary reflection
which seeks to deepen or extend it by a process of interpretation. This
means that knowledge is something more than 'beholding' the immediate data of sense and consciousness. It is not a static confrontation
with an object but a process of unfolding what is given in speech and
dialogue. In a sense, meaning is not spoken once but is always *being* spoken as one discourse interprets another: being is a continuous
self-explicating and self-unfolding in word and action. Reality itself is
a process of ceaseless translation and interpretation of one thing into
another.

For this reason discourse in the humanities can seem to have a
kind of endlessness to it. Indeed, one of the functions of myth and
symbol is to compensate for the poverty of discursive thinking by an-
ticipating the surplus or excess element of meaning that runs ahead
of our explicit conceptual formulations. Thus, poetic and symbolic
language is always on the way to full explication without ever quite
arriving. However, this should not be taken as having nihilistic or
skeptical implications; it is a function not of the paucity of intellect

but of the abounding richness of language and experience which always gives *more* than can be spoken at once. One can be in the dark from too much light or too little and our case is surely as Aristotle describes it: "our eyes are as those of bats in the light of the sun". From the standpoint of what I have called the metaphysics of interpretation it is idolatry to fix meaning to one simple essence or one privileged representation. It is idolatry, say, to reduce the language of religion to the statement of determinate fact. The images of mythology and religion are *always already* constituted by acts of interpretation and so of their very nature give rise to more of the same. No doubt, this is inherent in the reflexive nature of consciousness which always has within it the power to stand outside a given content and question or critically examine it. As Augustine pointed out long ago, the subject surpasses itself as object in each new act of reflection, its attention and will containing in the reflexive act a potential infinity of new knowledge as discourses give way to further discourses that surpass and comprehend them as sub-alternates.[35]

III

With this mind let us turn once again to the problem of religion. I will begin by laying out some basic distinctions. Humans, as far as I can ascertain, are religious animals. Obviously, I do not mean by this that that all people are consciously 'religious' but that religion lies at the foundation of all known cultures. The basic reason for this is that religion is our primary confrontation with that dimension of reality we might call 'the given'. By speaking of the 'given' I mean to indicate that a core aspect of religion is awe at and a sense of responsibility to something simply there. For instance, among the Sioux certain objects partake of an adjectival quality called *Wakan* that make them objects of reverence and respectful fear. In Islam, the *Koran* is taken to have an inimitable power of majesty and beauty that immediately authenticates its divine origin. In a Christian context, we might speak of the wisdom of God as manifested directly in the splendor of creation, as when in *Genesis* Yahweh pronounces his creation 'good'.

Now as humans are, as we have seen above, symbolic animals, these experiences of awe at the given are only the first moment of religion. The immediacy of reverence is a necessary but not sufficient condition for religion. The given is not 'there' without its mediation any more

---

[35] *The City of God* XI, 26.

than there is mediation without something given. Thus, human beings will inevitably express their awareness of the sacred in aesthetic
and symbolic forms such as poetry, sacred history and myth. What is
more, as human beings are political animals, our sense of the sacred
will always have as well a social and institutional expression. Thus,
religions have the features with which we are all familiar: visible authority structures, public rituals, symbolic and aesthetic forms, myths,
founding narratives etc. In short, symbolic and social mediation of the
given generates what we have loosely come to term 'organized religion'.
In point of fact, though, there is no 'unorganized' religion. Even Uni-
tarians must have parking lots. The reason for this is simple: events
do not attain discursive meaning for human beings outside of the given
structures of language, society and tradition. Grant to a feral child all
the ecstasies of St. Theresa and they would not amount to a religious
experience for the child could never *interpret* them without inherited
religious symbols or, say, traditions of mystical teaching embodied in
stories and texts.

Now if these were the only two elements of religion our job would
be simple.[36] Indeed, Dawkins himself rests at the very stage we have
reached in our inquiry: his frequently expressed awe at the beauty and
majesty of nature is mediated by the reflective knowledge contained
in the natural sciences and embodied in Western, liberal technocratic
social forms that guarantee the social authority of the sciences. By the
categories I am employing here, he is obviously a religious man though

---

[36] Alas religion is NOT an easy thing to study for empirically it presents an almost ungovernable diversity. Thus, it has proved almost impossible for scholars
of religion to decide on a definition for their subject matter. I have offered some
broad categories here that I hope are helpful though I admit they are as normative
as they are descriptive. The reader should note though that the moment of awe
can and often does atrophy, in which case religion begins to shade into *magic*.
Likewise the moment of mediation can atrophy in which case religion shades into
enthusiasm. Finally, the moments of awe and of spirit may atrophy in which case
religion falls into the vice of *formalism*. If we look at science we can see that as a
practice it does indeed have these three moments: is science then a sort of religion?
The reader may rightly feel that this stretches ordinary usage too far. I suggest,
though, that as human endeavors science and religion are closely analogous. Certainly, the one seems an outgrowth of the other: to see that this is so one might
(for example) contemplate the amount of basic *astronomical* data compiled by
priests and astrologers out of purely ritual or mystical interests. Franz Cumont's
Astrology among the Ancient Greeks and Romans is still a good read on this subject. A more recent account may be found in David C. Lindberg, *The Beginnings
of Western Science: The European Scientific Tradition in Philosophical, Religious
and Institutional Context, 600 B.C. to A.D. 1450* (Chicago: University of Chicago
Press, 1992), 13-20.

no doubt he would bristle at this attribution. Yet there is a third element to religious consciousness of which Dawkins seems blissfully unaware, no doubt because he has not yet attained to it with respect to his own cherished symbols: this is the negative or self-critical moment of religion that manifests itself in such endeavors as speculative theology, reforming zeal, mysticism, etc. Religious people not only create myths and symbols but smash them as well. Our primary experience of the 'given' externalizes itself in determinate forms but, from time to time, we can experience this as a limitation as much as a liberation. For instance, one of the strengths of myth is its high tolerance for contradiction and multiple and irreducible points of view: there is no problem for *mythos* as such in having, say, two stories of the flood. This makes it a very effective vehicle for registering the ambiguities and dualities of life. However, the speculative intelligence seeks some reconciliation of contrariety and opposition in a more comprehensive unity so that reflective culture seeks to overcome the immediacy of mythic consciousness: thus, we have the allegorizing of Homer by the Neo-Platonists or of the Christian scriptures by Origen or Augustine. What is more, we have a determined effort to translate imagery and narrative into speculative categories (as in the development of the doctrine of the trinity) or transcend it altogether via mystical experience (as in Plotinus, say).

Of course, readers familiar with the discourse of theology know that I am in some sense speaking of the Holy Spirit or third person of the Trinity: between the first moment of religion and the second lies a fissure or gap that the movement of a vital spiritual life will seek to equalize or overcome.[37] This movement is a return from external representation to the thing represented; a flight from the symbol to the symbolized or from the outer to the inner. Crucially, it is a movement of criticism *from within religion itself.* Thus, we have the movement

---

[37]Subtle readers will have noted that I have been talking about the Trinity all along both here and in the previous essay. It is far beyond the scope of this essay to fully explain this point but a close examination of great medieval thinkers such as Augustine, Eriugena and Bonaventure along with moderns such as Hegel or C. S. Pierce will show that the notion of the Trinity is one of the subtlest and most fruitful speculative concepts in the history of Western thought. For this reason, Dawkins makes a painful spectacle of himself when he mocks Trinitarian terms such as substance, nature and person (terms *demonstrably* lucid in themselves) as if they were so much gobbledygook. The best popular introduction to the speculative notion of the Trinity that I have found is the delightful essay "Scalene Trinities" by Dorothy L. Sayers (see *The Mind of the Maker* (London: Continuum International Publishing, 1994), 119-144).

in ancient Hebraism from sensuous representations of divine beings as natural powers to the conception of God as an utterly transcendent principle sovereign over a purely created order. Similarly we have in the New Testament a turn inward from an external principle of law to the free movement of love. In the Islamic religion we find a similar reversion from a destructive plurality of passions and worldly interests (the sin of *shirk*) to the inner freedom and peace embodied in the five pillars. Thus, we find that far from being un-revisable a number of major religions are in fact founded upon revolutionary change and consequently have a principle of reform and revision internal to themselves. Religion, insofar as it is *spiritual*, seeks an inward communion with the un-representable within representation, whether this be in the form of a mystical or contemplative union, a disciplined philosophical or theological meditation or practical works of love. As such, religious consciousness does rest satisfied at its second stage.

Thus, the critique of representation is as crucial to religion as representation itself for in it representation finds its truth and its purpose: the signs and symbols reveal by veiling and veil by revealing and thus have both a positive and negative dimension. Here, finally, after saying some rather harsh things, I can give Mr. Dawkins his due. I think I have shown to this point that both the mythic-symbolic and the intellectual and mystical belong to religious consciousness. The dichotomy between supposedly 'real' fundamentalist religion and the spurious pseudo-religion of 'sophisticated theology' is a false one. Each of these things is as vital an aspect of the history and nature of religion as the other: religion, if you like, is simultaneously above and below the level of literal fact. However, it would be perverse to deny that the scientific revolution has served a vital iconoclastic function in the evolution of Western religion. One thing one is struck by in a pre-modern writer like Augustine is the apparent casualness with which he can descend from the sublime heights of spiritual interpretation to explaining how Noah fit all the animals on the ark: the symbolic and realistic are fused to the point of confusion such that he can move blithely from one to the other and feel no strain between the two.[38] This is not, I suspect, because he was held in any way by our modern metaphysics of fact (as a contemporary fundamentalist might be). Rather, it seems as if he possessed the typically medieval notion that the sacred history recorded in scripture constituted a tissue of symbolic events so that the 'physical' ark was in just as real a sense the

---

[38] *The City of God* XV, 26-27.

church and the physical wood of it in just as real a sense the cross.

It is a great gain for *religious* consciousness when under the aegis of modern science nature and history are understood not simply as the expression of symbolic narrative but as having their own structure and intelligibility for this enables a clearer grasp of the *distinction* between symbols and the realities symbolized. Augustine himself in his *Confessions* and commentaries on *Genesis* admitted that the interpretation of scripture could not violate such universal and rational principles of order as the sciences could discover in nature for nature, especially in its mathematical aspects, was an expression of divine reason.[39] This allows us to purge traditional attitudes to scripture from any remaining taint of idolatry: it is a detraction from the significance of the story of the fall to wonder where it is set for of course it transpires everywhere and nowhere. For myth to know its own special mode of apprehension requires another contrasting mode of apprehension. For myth to know what it truly is and how it operates requires science. Until its overthrow by scientific rationalism mythic consciousness cannot know itself as such!

Thus, it is a move forward when the enlightenment traditions commended to us by Dawkins (and, I have no trouble admitting, deeply and genuinely valued by him) distinguish a factual realm of quantitative laws and their instantiations from the backdrop of mythic consciousness for there are all sorts of circumstances (like performing heart surgery) where this is a desirable substitution. However, science that does not serve life is an idol and the externalized mathematical abstractions of modern physics are, as Blake saw, a danger to the unity of life and the wholeness of persons if taken (simplistically) as a picture of reality as it is in itself. His violent reassertion of mythic thought against the 'unholy trinity' of 'Bacon, Locke and Newton' imparts an important reminder. The world of 'scientific fact' is a projection of a certain sort of thinking (and please note, this is NOT a criticism; there is nothing at all wrong with projections in themselves). This projection has the useful result for religion of revealing many traditional images of scripture to be just that: images. However, it offers only a partial liberation for the world of scientific objects is itself only an image of the totality; it is reality filtered through certain tools and techniques (and indeed filtered through certain metaphors and myths) that is capable of great local accuracy and precision but only at the cost of leaving many dimensions of experience out of account. Zo-

---

[39]See *Confessions* V, 8-10.

ology determines us to a certain understanding of dogs but the man who says the zoological dog is the 'real' dog and the dog of the pet owner (the dog as it is for affective relationships) is a sentimental illusion has committed a fundamental error. As H. G. Gadamer points out "...the truth that science states is itself relative to a particular attitude to the world and cannot at all claim to be the whole".[40] The world of natural attitudes and appearances is just as much a world as the 'being-in-itself' of scientific entities.

In other words, truth is not a matter of neutral, disengaged 'looking' at an 'already out there' set of facts and equations. Knowing is not 'taking a look'. Science, for perfectly understandable reasons, presents itself this way and presents the world it uncovers as the realm of determinate, objective 'out there' fact to which the subject simply submits (this, after all, is how the science game is played). However, truth is the totality: the 'truth' of science lies not simply in its description of the empirical world but in its social, ethical, political and even religious context without which it could not even begin to describe anything. The world of science is always *more* than the timeless, a-historical world of determinate fact and law it projects and there is no use complaining about this either. Again, as Gadamer points out, there is no science that has science or the scientist as its object: "the world of physics cannot be the whole of what exists. For even a world formula that contained everything, so that the observer of the system would also be included in the latter's equations, would still assume the existence of the physicist who, as calculator, would not be an object calculated."[41] Recognizing this fact opens us to the possibility of retrieving what is valuable in other stances such as the mythic or poetic for the world of science, like the world of poetry, is an *interpreted* world, a text whose parts must be understood in terms of the whole and vice versa. Being as *text* predetermines being as fact so that we are always already readers.

To conclude, Dawkins' disdain for theology seems to me to rest on a broader disdain for the interpretive culture of the Humanities and a hankering for the simple primary world of direct observation he takes to lie at the base of the sciences and to be the proper stance towards religious texts. Word directly mirrors thing so that science is reducible to fact and texts like the Bible are reducible to their most immediate and literal sense. The arguments of philosophers like Aquinas or Kant

---

[40]H. G. Gadamer, *Truth and Method* (New York, Seabury Press, 1975), 407.

[41]Gadamer, *Truth and Method*, 410.

can be apprehended directly without a consideration of context for an argument is nothing more than a detached and isolated bit of sense that works as well in summary as it does in the primary text. In short, he is an atomist who holds meaning to be reducible to its smallest components. I have tried (I hope successfully!) to present an alternate picture that makes our world more inhabitable by making mythic and symbolic modes (which still move millions of people) less alien and more human (humanizing the other being somewhat important to a global society!). This picture is based not on the model of looking but on that of reading: myths and narratives and symbols and rituals in religion, as much as models, analogies and heuristic metaphors in science are pre-anticipations of the whole to which we approximate more and more completely the more consciously and fully we actualize their meaning by acts of interpretation. We do not simply look at the world but elicit meaning from it by a process of discussion, reflection and dialogue, truth and reality being the terminal point of this process. It is my contention that this model of understanding truth and knowledge makes richer sense of both religion and science than either Dawkins' positivism or its fundamentalist other ever can though whether this is so I leave to the reader to decide.

5

BELIEFS AND EVIDENCE: IS FAITH A VICE?

Normally one should not write about books one dislikes. Life is short and time is usually misspent in rubbishing the work of others. I will be honest with my readers: for its bombast, the coarseness of its sensibility and its lack of rigorous argumentation I found Sam Harris' *The End of Faith* a difficult book to finish. Nevertheless, I have decided to swallow my distaste and say a few words about it. For one thing many intelligent people have read it and have reacted as favorably to its thesis as to its style. Moreover, Harris' tome has sold well and won prestigious prizes. It has won a following among people who are no lovers of bombast and poor argumentation and this, no doubt, is because it is a vigorous defense of ideas they cherish. Persons I have asked about it have told me that while it is a somewhat simplistic book (perhaps) its defense of enlightenment ideals is timely and important. What is more, there is a legitimate frustration on the part of many intellectuals with the virulent culture of fundamentalism and Harris gives vivid expression to this mood. Thus, we may credit Mr. Harris with hitting the nerve in a tooth which needs repairing if not total extraction. Belief and justification *are* crucial issues where mistakes can have deadly consequences and we ought to examine their nature with all due diligence and care. Faith (understood in the broadest sense as *pistis* or opinion concerning the non-evident) is, in my view, intrinsic to the human condition. As such it seems to me folly to speak of 'ending' it. As Augustine often pointed out you have to *believe* your teachers about the times tables before you can actually know them; however, this does not mean we can exercise no critical control over it. A discussion of the nature and role of faith in human affairs will, by determining its scope, also define its limits.

Accordingly, I will consider the key issue raised by Mr. Harris: whether faith is an epistemic vice. On this issue, the second chapter 'The Nature of Belief' proves surprisingly useful, if perhaps not quite in the way its author intended. In this section Mr. Harris articulates views on the nature of belief and especially on the nature of reasonable belief that are so clearly and cleverly articulated and so completely and demonstrably wrong that they constitute a rare opportunity for teaching. Here is Sam Harris on belief: "believing a given proposition is a matter of believing that it faithfully represents some state of the world, and this fact yields some immediate insights into the standards by which our beliefs should function. In particular, it reveals why we cannot help but value evidence and demand that propositions about the world logically cohere".[42] Beliefs, he continues, are principles of action "...whatever they may be at the level of the brain they are processes by which our understanding (and *mis*understanding) of the world is represented and made available to guide our behavior".[43] Deeply (perhaps unduly) impressed by the law of non-contradiction, Harris adds that the propositions we believe entail or exclude each other in the same way facts in the world do and must have some measure of systematic coherence if they are to represent the world effectively. What is more, he holds that for this to happen reliably and effectively it must be the case that physical neural events in the brain mirror the laws of logic and probability that govern the world.[44]

But how do we know when our beliefs and the brain events that underlie them have effectively mirrored the world? Harris is a little sketchier here but it seems that we rely once again on those twin warhorses verification and falsification: true beliefs are those we have empirically verified and meaningful beliefs are those for which we can specify falsifying instances. Never mind for now that the notion of fal-

---

[42]Sam Harris, *The End of Faith: Religion, Terror, and the Future of Reason* (New York: W. W. Norton & Co., 2005), 51.

[43]Harris, *The End of Faith*, 52.

[44]Harris, *The End of Faith*, 58. Science does not sort as easily with logic as Harris thinks. Standard accounts of hypothetico-deductive method (verifying hypotheses through observation) are highly problematic given that the formal statement of H/D, if p then q, but q therefore p commits the fallacy of affirming the consequent. Wesley Salmon ruefully notes a quip by Morris R. Cohen to the effect that "...a text book in logic is divided into two parts; in the first part (on deduction) the fallacies are explained, while in the second part (on induction) they are committed." (Salmon, 5)

sification was introduced by Popper because he regarded the theory of verification as a failure: Harris will have it all ways at once. Thus, he says: "science is science because it represents our most committed effort to verify that our statements about the world are true (or at least not false). We do this by observation and experiment within the context of theory".[45] Below he adds (in apparent defiance of David Hume) that "given a sufficient number of verifiable statements, plucked from the ethers of Papal vision, we could begin speaking seriously about any further claims Jesus might make. The point is that his authority would be derived in the only way that such authority ever is- *by making claims about the world that can be corroborated by future observation*".[46] However, in spite of this unreconstructed positivism, we find another passage where Harris tries on his Popperian hat: "...the engineer says the bridge will hold; the doctor says the infection is resistant to penicillin- these people have defeasible reasons for their claims about the way the world is. The mullah, the priest and the rabbi do not. Nothing could change about this world, or about the world of their experience, that could demonstrate the falsity of many of their core beliefs".[47] Thus, brain events can reliably be known to mirror the world when falsifiable statements are verified by repeated observation.

So far all is good in the Eden of observation and evidence. Sadly though, there is a snake in the garden. As though they had never read Ayer or Popper there is a whole class of believers (religious ones) who assert propositions that can neither be verified nor falsified! Thus are we introduced to the eponymous villain of the piece 'faith'. Faith, we find out, is a "belief in, and life orientation towards, certain historical and metaphysical propositions".[48] Below we find out that religious faith in particular is "simply *unjustified* belief in matters of ultimate concern...".[49] If we were in doubt before about faith being a bad thing then this should settle it. A belief that is unjustified is not one we should hold and since (it seems) that any belief is a religious belief if it is held without justification in a matter of ultimate concern then surely no one should hold any. Cavilers might ask if this isn't question begging: surely whether people who hold Christian, Jewish or Muslim beliefs are *justified* in doing so is the very point at issue and not even a man as clever as Sam Harris can win an argument by def-

[45] Harris, *The End of Faith*, 76.
[46] Harris, *The End of Faith*, 77; my italics.
[47] Harris, *The End of Faith*, 66.
[48] Harris, *The End of Faith*, 65.
[49] Harris, *The End of Faith*, 65.

68

inition. However, I am happy to regard this as a slip: surely what Harris *means* to say is that religious beliefs are typically held without *good* justification because they are poorly supported by observation and are un-falsifiable. In short, motivated by wishful thinking we believe certain historical and metaphysical propositions which we cannot properly verify.

Make no mistake either; Harris is no fan of wishful thinking, which he seems to regards as a vicious moral fault. At this point our philosopher turns scold "... the fact that unjustified beliefs can have a consoling influence on the human mind is no argument in their favor...".[50] Further down we read that "evidence (whether sensory or logical) is the only thing that suggests that a given belief is about the world. We have names for people who have many beliefs for which there is no rational justification. When their beliefs are extremely common we call them 'religious'; otherwise they are likely to be called 'mad', 'psychotic' or 'delusional'".[51] Yet even the religious know that their brain states must mirror the world at some point for propositional truth about the world is the only 'logical space' that belief can occupy: "I cannot say, however, 'I believe in God because it is prudent to do so'... Of course I can *say* this, but I cannot mean by the word believe what I mean when I say things like 'I believe that water is really two parts hydrogen and one part oxygen because two centuries of physical experiments attest to this...'".[52] It is because of this ingrained necessity for evidence that religious people leap at tales of the miraculous for they seem to supply the kind of evidence they really want for their beliefs. Miracles offer us in the desert of uncertainty "... a cool drink of data".[53]

What to make of all this epistemological dogma? Shall I point out once again that religious beliefs have a supra-propositional symbolic element? Shall I point out that many scientific beliefs do as well? Shall I bring attention to the fact that hardly any theologian of any merit thinks the proposition 'God exists' is of the same type and order as 'water is two parts hydrogen and one part oxygen'? Shall I point out the difficulty of conceiving how brain events 'mirror' the world?[54]

---

[50]Harris, *The End of Faith*, 68.
[51]Harris, *The End of* Faith, 72.
[52]Harris, *The End of Faith*, 62.
[53]Harris, *The End of Faith*, 66.
[54]Brain events may, of course, correspond to events in the world but in what sense is that correspondence a 'mirroring'? Stabbing my foot with a sharp poker sends a signal to my brain but the neurochemical events that then transpire are

There are a host of problems that could be raised with Harris' account but I will confine myself to what I think are the two essential points. Firstly, I do not think that evidence is confined to empirical confirmation. Secondly, I do not think that justification is in every case evidential. In others words, direct or experimental observation is not the only kind of evidence and evidence is not the only kind of justification. As these two principles are the lynchpin of Harris' claim that faith is an epistemic vice attacking them will bring the rest of the edifice crumbling down. In the course of this I hope to show that there are in fact several analogous kinds of belief and that justification and evidence vary according to these different kinds. I hold this to be a useful exercise for while few philosophers will express themselves as incautiously as Mr. Harris does I suspect that many of them might share his underlying attitude. Whatever philosophers may think of direct realism and the correspondence theory of truth, and however much the verification principle may have fallen out of favor many of them (I suspect) *do* find something funny about religious beliefs and if pressed to say what this was might well say it had to do with the fact that they are not justified in the way scientific beliefs are and so seem not to be justified at all. Perhaps the ethical theory of utilitarianism offers an analogous case; the discursive theory laid out by Mill and his successors is so beset with difficulties that few will really defend it as a theory. Nonetheless, deep in their bones many people are quite convinced that morality must have something to do with consequences. Accordingly, I shall attempt to outline an account of belief, evidence and justification that will show this attitude to be excessively narrow and restrictive and will allow for an intellectually responsible approach to the broad range of our beliefs. So now I will move on to our consideration of belief. I will outline several sorts of belief and the forms of justification appropriate to them. My account will be somewhat oversimplified and schematic; forms of evidence and justification are not quite so neatly separable in reality as I am going to present them here. However, I hope that my little outline is adequate to the larger point I am making.

II

A good many of the things we believe can be stated in simple propositional form. Beliefs which can be stated in this way are also

---

hardly a representation of a poker stabbing a foot (ie. A physical description of them would not be a description of a stabbing motion).

open to a simple form of justification. A justification is a motive for belief given in the form of a reason. For instance, I may have a *motive* for believing that my neighbor is a thief: I may despise my neighbor and wish her ill and consequently desire to believe the absolute worst I can about her. However, this motive for my belief is not a reason. Usually, if I have a jaundiced attitude towards someone I will try to find some ground over and above my dislike of her to make damaging assertions about her character. Thus, I will try to catch her in the act of thievery or look for some other indirect form of evidence for her thefts so that I may utter the proposition 'my neighbor Sally is a thief'. This proposition is subject to the law of non-contradiction: Sally is not and cannot be a thief and non-thief at the same time and in the same respect. She is either a thief or not one. Furthermore the justification of my assertion is an identifiable act of theft on Sally's part: we must either observe Sally steal or point to observations that allow us to infer that Sally has stolen. Here our language *seems* to mirror events in a fairly uncomplicated way and our goal really does seem to be matching a proposition in our heads to a state of affairs. Of course, this is a bit too innocent. I do not, strictly speaking, ever see Sally steal. I may see Sally get in my car and drive away but to call this stealing of course requires some developed moral categories (what if she is taking the car because of an emergency?) and some fairly abstract notions like personal identity and property. What is more, if I take Sally to court I find a little more of my innocence tarnished for I soon realize that the judge is not really trying to determine whether Sally stole a car but whether *on a balance of probabilities* or *beyond a reasonable doubt* she did so and this is not quite the same thing.

Still, there are many situations where any such pre-formation of my judgments is so far in the background that one might as well, for all practical purposes, say that we confirm or disconfirm propositions by *direct observation*. If I am wondering if there is beer in the fridge I open the fridge and look and if this is not simply a matter of pure observation, i.e. it involves certain assumptions about the reliability of my senses under certain conditions, ideas about the nature of space, etc., my quest for beer does not generally involve me in much reflection on these. Simple empirical propositions *are as if* they were confirmed or disconfirmed by direct observation and that is the sort of justification appropriate to them. Now the proposition mentioned above about Sally's thievery is a bit more complicated; even a direct observation of Sally's act of theft involves us in some theoretical construction in the sphere of ethics and if nobody has seen her steal my car but a judge has to reconstruct the best story about what happened to it then direct observation has been replaced by *interpretive reasoning* (in one of its most basic forms) and this is the chief way in which we justify our beliefs about events in the past which cannot be directly observed.

Now we are alas some way from the garden. We began with uncomplicated propositions about the world that could be justified (more or less) by observation and moved on to more complex propositions whose meaning depended on theoretical construction and whose justification lay in an interpretive reconstruction of past events. Already we can see that there are at least two kinds of beliefs (about the present and the past) which have two distinct kind of justification (observation and interpretation). Now there is a third kind that has yet another sort of justification and that is belief concerning generalities. I may say to myself not 'William is honest' but 'honesty is the best policy' and this is a general proposition whose justification lies in being a sound induction from a number of instances of honest people prospering. Thus, we have beliefs about general patterns whose justification lies in *inductive reasoning*. What is more, should I want to get some way back to the paradise of observation there is a further technique: I might try to take some of my interpretive stories about the world and deduce consequences from them that I can test by observation. This gives me not only knowledge of the past and present but some purchase on what will happen in the future. Thus, I have some beliefs about the future course of events whose justification lies in *experimental reasoning*.

Now observation, induction and experimental reasoning are what we might call evidential justifications. Interpretive reason offers justification that is not simply evidential (evidence for it is pointing to the meaning of signs) but appeals also to our sense of the coherence and economy of events: it offers to us some whole that we accept because it is plausible and satisfying. I fear though, that I have hardly scratched the surface of our beliefs for so far I have dealt with beliefs expressed in propositions that purport to describe the world. There are whole other sets of beliefs which do not quite do this. Many of us believe that electrons orbit the nucleus of an atom the way planets orbit the Sun and this belief is not false but it is not literally true either: it is a model for understanding something that cannot be directly pictured by our imaginations. It is not a proposition that mirrors the world but an image or analogy that helps us order our thoughts about the world because being human we find it difficult to think without some kind of picture of what we are thinking about. Nor is it easy to make significant discoveries without heuristic aids to guide us of which models and analogies are prime examples; in the same way an 18th century philosopher might have tried to understand a problem in anthropology or politics by thinking of man in the state of nature. Now it matters little how literally an early modern philosopher believed in the state of nature; it matters little how literally a modern person believes in the orbital model of the atom. However they are consciously conceived their purpose is to serve as functional analogies or heuristic models and their justification lies their fruitfulness: the notion of a state of nature is justified to the extent that it allows a Hobbes or Locke or Rousseau to attain novel and satisfying insights into the nature of society and the central problems of politics. Thus we have beliefs halfway between the literal and purely metaphorical whose justification lies in the results they generate.[55]

The generalizations we uncover through induction and experiment are often organized into more or less coherent wholes called theories. Thus a biologist may believe in evolution or an astronomer in the heliocentric theory of the solar system. Belief in a theory does not seem to be the same thing as belief in a fact. Propositional statements of fact are intended to describe specific things and events but a theory does not describe the world by picturing or representing the facts in it directly. There is no Archimedean point at which one can stand and see the earth revolving around the sun and as far as describing the observed phenomena of the solar system goes any number of theories may do so in an empirically-adequate fashion. Indeed, a potential infinity of theoretical constructs can describe a particular data set. If one lived in the 16th century there was little to choose empirically between the systems of Copernicus and Tycho Brahe. As mere 'pictures'

---

[55] Readers interested in the question of metaphor in science may begin with Mary Hesse's seminal book *Models and Analogies in Science* (Notre Dame: University of Notre Dame Press, 1970). Hesse points out that "Men are seen to be more like wolves after the wolf metaphor is used and wolves seem to be more human. Nature becomes more like a machine in the mechanical philosophy, and actual concrete machines are seen as if stripped down to their essential qualities of mass and motion" (p. 163). Hesse's point here is that metaphors are not reducible to primary data because they interact with their empirical content to produce new and unforeseen insights and descriptions: their function is *structural* and *constitutive* as much as it is descriptive. Shakespeare, for instance, does not just describe political authority using metaphors of commerce and agriculture but illuminates its nature and for Hesse scientific metaphors do much the same, though in a more rigorously circumscribed way than their poetic counterparts.

both were adequate to account for the known facts for both managed to include more or less the same data in their respective representations. Yet Copernicus' heliocentric theory was judged superior to the Tychonian scheme (where the planets revolved around the sun which in turn revolved around the earth) because the latter had a displeasingly arbitrary *ad hoc* character to it. Thus theories which succeed must be doing more than merely 'picturing' things: as theoretical constructs they must serve a multitude of other functions and conform to a multiplicity of basic aims. They must tell an explanatory story offering a reasonable fit with observed data and they must do so with as much economy and elegance as possible. They must also be productive of new insights and advances both theoretical and practical. They may even need to conform to political, social or religious aims. A theory in biology or genetics that supports the equality of the sexes or races is obviously better for *us* than one that doesn't. Racist or sexist theories are a waste of time for reasons that are political before they are scientific. This polyvalent nature of scientific theories of course leaves much room for debate about the nature and role of truth in the sciences: realists strongly defend the notion of objective 'out there' truth, while instrumentalists, anti-realists and constructivists hold the aim of science to be not truth, but utility, empirical adequacy, vitalistic/pragmatic imperatives or some other comparable goal.[56] Nonetheless, it is clear that theories do far more work than just 'picturing' things.

Thus, theories are beliefs about the relationship between the general patterns found in observation founded partly on observational accuracy and partly on other values. If you like, a theory is a belief not about observational facts but about relationships between facts and its justification lies partly in its fit with data and partly in its own inherent qualities of coherence, scope, parsimony, fruitfulness, etc. Ultimately, this is because a theory states a set of purely intellectual

---

[56]The literature on this question is huge and technically-daunting. The present author has tried to hew to a moderate constructivism such as he thinks can be grounded in the tradition of Plato and his successors but of course any position taken here is bound to be controversial. Readers, alas, must tackle these questions for themselves. Fundamental places to begin are Thomas Kuhn's *Structure of Scientific Revolutions* and Paul Feyerabend's more Nietzschean account of science in *Against Method*. It is a curious feature of humanists like Dawkins and Harris that they not only endorse a strong realist position on the nature of science (which is their right) but assume it with little or no argument. Indeed, they write as if debates which have been going on for five decades or more have never even occurred.

or intelligible relations between things to which, of course, the 'facts' are never quite adequate. In a real sense it does not describe facts at all but noetic relations between them and so theoretical propositions are not true in the way factual ones are. They are not mirrors that reflect back passively the empirically-*given* in a naïve or immediate way but are active frameworks that organize the world for us in intellectually-satisfying and useful ways.[57] Belief in a theory is belief in the beautiful, the useful and the good as much as in the true. Thus, belief in evolution is not belief of the same sort as belief in the presence of milk in my fridge. Perhaps Galileo[58] was getting at this when he said that in science nature is *made* to speak the language of reason: the function of science is as much to tidy up the messy imprecision of the empirical world as to reflect it! Of course this, as I have noted above, leaves the question of the 'correspondence' of theoretical entities to the real world somewhat up in the air: as Plato might have said, the sciences are *dianoetic*, or formalistic constructions of the understanding that do not comprehend their ultimate grounds and so do not attain to full knowledge of the true, the beautiful or the good but rather offer us various images or likenesses of it.[59]

We can see that beliefs in theories and models are partly evidential in character, partly pragmatic or instrumental and partly interpretive. If you like, they combine interpretive, pragmatic, experimental, and observational forms of justification. Now we have a number of beliefs that are not observational or directly or even indirectly evidential. Thus, we believe in the uniformity and stability of nature, the existence of other minds, the reality of the external world, the freedom of the will, etc. We rarely doubt these things outside of philosophy class but proving them is notoriously difficult. We might call these basic beliefs and the reasons we hold them are (usually) pragmatic. Take

---

[57]In fact, as Feyerabend points out, data do not and cannot generate theories: "one answer which is no longer as popular as it used to be is that science works by collecting facts and inferring theories from them. The answer is unsatisfactory as theories never *follow from* facts in the strict logical sense. To say that they may yet be *supported* from the facts assumes a notion of support that A. does not show this defect; and B. is sufficiently sophisticated to permit us to say to what extent, say, the theory of relativity is supported by the facts. No such notion exists today..." (p. 221). This observation is borne out by the fact that theories are not generated by facts at all. Often they are *created* by leaps of the imagination and then, by experimentation or some other form of testing, brought into some kind of relation with the data.

[58]*Dialogue concerning the Two Chief World Systems* trans. Stillman Drake (1967: University of California Press, 328).

[59]*Republic* VI, 511.

the case of other minds. At a certain point in our early childhood we no doubt drew little or no distinction between our thoughts, desires, interests, etc. and those of other people. Other people were real only in relation to us. However, tensions between our needs and those of others inevitably arise and we are faced with a choice: to continue seeing the other person as extensions of ourselves or effect a revolution in our point of view and begin to regard them as persons in their own right equivalent to ourselves. In other words, we can begin to look at the world ethically, and if we do we find the richer possibilities it affords in terms of our own growth more than justify taking this stance. Thus, basic beliefs are most often held on the basis of their *pragmatic value* and not on the basis of observation or inference. If it is true that there is some inference involved in this belief (something I doubt) it is only an inference we make if we see that it is pragmatically worthwhile to do so; it can never force itself upon us unwillingly and that is why we have psychopaths and people with narcissistic personality disorders.

We also have aesthetic and moral beliefs. I believe that Bach is a great composer and the assassination of Martin Luther King a heinous crime. Neither of these propositions state contingent facts about the world but describe certain things in the world as beautiful or good or their opposites. Such judgments are not founded on observation or evidence; they are not quite founded on interpretive reasoning either (though this no doubt plays a role) nor are they justified entirely in terms of their results. Aesthetic and ethical judgments are justified by our educated sense of moral and artistic things: in other words they are judged by *prudence*. A musical education involving wide listening, critical reading, discussion and practice will form in us (in most cases) a developed taste, an ingrained habit of appreciation which we can consult when we need to make judgments on a work of music. Similarly, as Aristotle pointed out, the practice and habit of moral virtue will give us an ingrained sense of where the limits of right and wrong lie in behavior. The more we practice virtue the better judges of it we become so that we can perceive the right thing to do (more often than not) in the particular circumstances we face. Many arts and crafts are like this as well; a good general, like Napoleon, who has deeply internalized the military art, can deal with many unforeseen situations to which no preset rules of strategy or tactics can be applied. Thus, there are many beliefs we have whose justification rests on educated habit and affinity for some sphere of activity. These beliefs differ markedly from scientific ones for they concern not generalities but the judgment of singulars; Nelson was a great admiral because he perceived that the standard rules of naval tactics *did not* apply to the specific situation of the battle of Trafalgar.

We have many beliefs whose justification lies in the affective side of the human person. Thus, there are many things we judge by means of our faculty of empathy. People who are incapable of feeling compassion for humans (or animals for that matter) are poor judges of social situations and behavior. Certain tendencies in Western philosophy have inclined us, almost reflexively, to distinguish knowing from feeling and of course there are all kinds of instances where our emotions must be put aside to see a situation clearly. However there are other instances where this is the precise opposite of what we should do. A pained look on a friend's face at something I have said may be easy to dismiss rationally as 'no big deal' but my feeling of discomfort and awkwardness is probably one I should listen to. Of course, as Aristotle would point out, feelings *per se* are not a guide to action but the feelings of a well-balanced, mature individual *are* in fact a kind of light that can guide judgment. The *educated* person (in the moral sense) is one who can trust his or her own feelings and appetites because they are integrated into a well-structured personhood.[60]

Many beliefs are of a purely pragmatic character and can be held *against* beliefs of an observational, experimental or interpretive kind. A mother who is searching for her missing son does not measure the intensity of her search by a calculation of the likelihood of success. The objective grounds for hope may be quite slim but it does not follow that, as a rational person, the mother in question is obligated to scale back her efforts accordingly. Nor is she obligated to measure her optimism by a calculus of the odds: she is absolutely right to believe her son will be found regardless (at least up to the point when she begins to do grave harm to herself or others). Similarly, a doctor suffering from cancer may have a dim view (qua doctor) of his chances. However, as a patient he is entitled to quite another view: pessimism, no matter how realistic, is a poor place from which to fight a disease so there is little point in the doctor taking any but the most cheerful view possible under the circumstances. Thus, there are instances where the demands of life justify certain beliefs quite apart from their epistemic value.

I could go on with many more examples of differing sorts of beliefs having differing justifications (I could speak of mathematical and log-

---

[60] *Nichomachean Ethics* III, 11, 119, 10.

ical beliefs or beliefs based on authority or trust, etc.) but I believe my point has been made. A belief can rest on any of several grounds whether observational, experimental, interpretive, pragmatic, prudential, affective or other. A wise or knowing person is not only one who knows according to one of these modes but is practiced in knowing *which* form of justification is appropriate to which sort of question in which circumstance. A husband who seeks observational evidence of his wife's fidelity is in most circumstances an ass. A scientist who seeks to prove the existence of God experimentally is a theological innocent. A woman who will not believe in evolution until she sees it happening before her eyes does not know what theoretical knowledge is and how it is justified. We can see, then, that Mr. Harris' equation of reasonable belief with empirical propositions verified observationally is a drastic oversimplification and that he has, by these means, scarcely laid a glove to any significant religious belief. Certainly, there seems at this point all kinds of 'logical space' for 'faith' to hide in for at best he has excluded from it only one kind of evidence and only one kind of justification.

III

It now remains to apply some of what we have learned to examples of religious belief to see whether they are amenable to justification in the broader sense we have laid out. In the second essay of this volume I discussed my own belief in God and indicated the sorts of considerations appropriate to justifying that belief. Here I will pick another example. Listen to Mr. Harris on the Roman Catholic doctrine of transubstantiation: "consider", he says, "one of the cornerstones of the Catholic faith... Jesus Christ- who, as it turns out, was born of a virgin, cheated death (sic!), and rose bodily into the heavens- can now be eaten in the form of a cracker. A few Latin words spoken over your favorite Burgundy, and you can drink his blood as well. Is there any doubt that a lone subscriber to these beliefs would be considered mad? Rather, is there any doubt that he would *be* mad? The danger of religious faith is that it allows otherwise normal human beings to reap the fruits of madness and consider them holy".[61] Well, we can see that Mr. Harris takes a dim view of the 'cornerstone' of the Catholic religion even without that cheeky substitution of 'cracker' for the correct term 'host'. But by this point in the essay I hope we have learned to ask of belief in transubstantiation (as of any other belief) 'what sort of

---

[61]Harris, *The End of Faith*, 73.

belief is it?' and 'how is a belief of this type justified?'. Harris seems to take it as a literal propositional belief (which it may or may not turn out to be) and judges it accordingly. However, I wish to spend a few paragraphs considering Harris' star instance of religious madness a bit more closely to see if this is so.

Now most Christians have some belief that Christ is present in some fashion in the central ritual of communion however they may describe or decline to describe the manner of that presence. I am not interested in the doctrinal controversies over this matter but only, if I may use the expression, in the phenomenology of the belief. So, there are many Christian forms of the belief in the so called 'real presence'. The Roman Catholic church has a certain way of describing this presence; to cite the Council of Trent: "because Christ our redeemer said that it was truly his body that he was offering under the species of bread it has always been the conviction of the church... that by the consecration of the bread and wine a change takes place in which the whole substance of bread is changed into the substance of the body of Christ our Lord and the whole substance of the wine into the substance of his blood. This change the holy Catholic Church fittingly and properly names transubstantiation"[62] Well, the first way in which this belief could be understood is as a literal propositional assertion. Harris would have it so and so, I suppose, would at least some of the devout. However, consideration of some of the terminology used in this definition might lead us to wonder whether this is quite the case. The definition speaks of a change of some kind but it is not a change of the sort we ordinarily observe. Indeed, there is no *observed* change at all. The 'species' or visible presentation of bread and wine remains unchanged so on the phenomenal level there is no event at all. The proposition 'bread changed into flesh' in its ordinary empirical sense means that the visible accidents of bread disappeared and were replaced by the visible accidents of flesh. So, the definition given above does not ask Catholics to believe anything contrary to what their senses report but asserts a change of 'substance', of inner identity rather than external appearance. With no visible alteration the *activity* manifested by the accidents has altered but not the accidents themselves: under the visible species of bread and wine there is no longer the action of chemical compounds, atoms and electrons but the action of Christ offering himself to us and to God.

This transformation of the underlying activity from the action of

---

[62] *The Church Teaches*, 722, p. 283.

physical matter to the action of self-sacrificing love is called transubstantiation for one substance (i.e underlying activity), is said to become another without, if you will tolerate a neologism, *transaccidation*. Note though, that the definition speaks of this not as a literally accurate description but as a fitting and proper description. I think there is a rationale for this apparent hesitation. The fathers of Trent *did not* want to assert a contradictory phenomenal appearance like a burning bush; there is nothing magical or superstitious here. They did, though, want to assert an alteration in the significance or meaning of the phenomenal presentation: the bread and wine were to become nothing more and nothing less than efficacious signs of God's love for humanity and of the presence of that love here and now among the worshipers gathered in his name. The notion of a change of substance without a change of accidents was judged (rightly or wrongly) to be the most fitting way to indicate this (for something changes and something doesn't) but it is no more a literal description of 'what happens' than the orbital model of the atom or the billiard ball model of the behavior of gases. Of course the temptation with models and analogies is to take them literally and to mistake the medium for the message (as it were). I am sure many people have understood transubstantiation in a grossly literal sense just as many people think electrons literally orbit protons or that genes literally contain the traits that express them. However, the belief is not, as far as I can make out, originally intended as a literal propositional assertion.

But why believe in transubstantiation as opposed to something else or nothing at all? What type of justification can such a belief be given? On one level the answer given above is authority: we believe in transubstantiation because Christ (who ought to know!) says 'this is my body'. However, this is a dead, external way to believe anything and if one has moved from a passage of scripture to a technical definition using terms drawn from Aristotle there is an obvious grasp at understanding what one has been told to believe. Now in the sciences one of the motives for believing or disbelieving anything is coherence: the reason I do not think to ask whether fermentation is caused by fairies is not because I have observed their absence from my still. Nobody to my knowledge (and I am prepared to stand corrected!) has ever tested for their presence and achieved a negative result. No, the reason I do not consider the hypothesis that fermentation is caused by fairies is that this would isolate fermentation from other chemical processes; as an explanation it would not fit with other explanations and my world would be less coherent and unified. Thus, congruence or lack thereof is a motive for belief or disbelief. Similarly, the motive for believing in something like transubstantiation is its congruence with other core Christian or Catholic beliefs. In fact, the reason the Catholic Church believes in transubstantiation is that it *believes in what it is doing in the mass.*

This takes a bit of unpacking. I am an avid enthusiast (and a somewhat halting practitioner) of the art of poetry. Consequently, I am a little mystified when people of a rationalist bent say that the notion of transubstantiation is unintelligible or when people of piety say it is a deep incomprehensible mystery. To me it seems the most ordinary thing in the world for as far as I can tell transubstantiation is just what any poet is trying to effect when he or she makes one thing reveal the nature of another. Shakespeare, in his famous sonnet, is attempting (unsuccessfully!) to make that summer's day reveal, not itself, but the beauty of his beloved. The more powerful the symbol employed the more fully and completely it ceases to be itself and the more fully and completely the thing symbolized is present through it. What the Catholic Church believes in by believing in transubstanti- ation is the power of its symbols to effect what they signify: natural signs and events can be *sacraments* or signs that reveal spiritual events that transcend them. To use an example from Plato, a cloak can be a cloak or it can be Peter or John or Sally's cloak and this makes all the difference to how we regard it if Peter, John or Sally are, say, dead or in some way absent.

For example, I once read the story of a Columbian saint who would always sit on the sunny side of a certain square in Cartagena because that was the side on which the African slaves were condemned to sit. Now sitting is a gesture that signifies a certain natural desire such as a desire for repose. Sitting on the *shady* side of the square signifies a natural desire to avoid the excessive heat of the sun. However what does sitting on the sunny side signify? Why should somebody deliber- ately renounce a privilege that his society afforded him and indentify instead with the despised and excluded? Why should somebody act contrary to the desires nature has implanted in him for his own ben- efit? Why should he do so on behalf of people his society tells him are non-persons and thus none of his kin or kind? Well, ignoring for now the *ad hoc* explanations one could contrive to cover a case like this, let us say the saint in question was motivated by charity: beyond all impulse of nature and beyond all rational calculation he identified himself with the other by an unconstrained impulse of love. Existing in one world, with its hierarchies and constraints, he, by a free gift of love, created another. The natural act of sitting became then a sign of something *supernatural* or freely creative without natural antecedent: something that signified nature in one context now signifies something divine without any disruption or alteration of the senses. The saint has, by this simple act, affected a sort of transubstantiation.

So, the belief in transubstantiation boils down to a belief that natural acts can signify the unconstrained power of love. Of course, there is no discursive path to believing in such a power. I cannot prove to anyone that Columbian saints are motivated by *agape* as opposed to hyper-subtle self-interest. I cannot prove even to myself that any act of mine proceeds from a like principle. On one level, belief that charity is a real power in the world is a sort of faith. However, I cannot quite regard it as 'unjustified belief' for the belief in unconditional love has altered the world in incalculable ways and is a sort of watershed behind which we can no longer really go. A world in which a slave, or a leper or a criminal is a potential object of unreserved love every bit as much as an artist, philosopher or business man is a different world than any ancient people inhabited but it is, in an utterly inescapable way, our world for all our notions of equality and human rights are ultimately grounded in it. Charity is the foundational principle of any civilization we wish to call Western even as law is the foundation of Islamic civilization and all that seems alien and repulsive to us in other cultures is so because of our implicit commitment to this principle. There is faith on a purely personal level and this can be as subjective and arbitrary as Mr. Harris pleases but 'civilizational faith' is another thing altogether. It is the core assumption of a way of life (exactly as belief in the validity of sense knowledge is a pragmatic assumption of science) whose manifestations range all the way from Christian liturgy to how we treat homosexuals, prisoners or people of alien races.

Perhaps I can put it this way: life is a kind of gamble on what sort of world is worth living in. Christian faith, with all its attendant symbols and stories, is a sort of gamble that loving unconditionally the most difficult of our neighbors will bring about the kingdom of God. The love I show any individual may be cruelly betrayed time and time again. The quest for justice and peace may be betrayed time and again by pettiness, spite and self-interest. Certainly, if we go on loving people and striving for justice on a personal or social level it is no doubt partly because we sense that a society founded on knowing cynicism would be colder and crueler even than the one we presently struggle with. A world of ideals subverted and betrayed is bad enough but a world with none at all would be hell. Yet over and above this we surely hold (at least implicitly) that goodness has genuine force or power in this world and that the triumph of evil is never simply pre-ordained. Thus, we *act as if* the good must make a difference quite apart from whether we can justify this attitude empirically. The least good thing we do is an act of faith in the possibility of a better world. Our particular gamble in the Western world (which makes it look crazed and anarchic to other societies) is that that community and its obligations is ultimately consistent with the free, untrammeled development of human personality. We *do not* act on the assumption that life is a tragic contradiction but that basic goods can be reconciled and surely this rests not on experience or observation (which is forever confirming the opposite) but on the conviction (however un-thematic) that however slowly, however painfully, the good will win out and we are not defeated from the outset by the limitations of the human condition. This is not a rational faith if by rational I mean that it can be justified inductively or deductively; however, I am sure most of us would agree that it is the faith of reasonable people in *our* world. Thus, the belief that the ideal can be and indeed is in some sense the actual, while expressed in Catholic liturgy in a form that sounds peculiar to outsiders, has many other expressions as well and is, indeed, the founding principle of any progressive society.

To conclude, a belief in transubstantiation is cognate to any number of other core Western values and can be recognized as such by anyone whether they have the faintest religious belief or not. It is thus as sane or insane as our civilization itself. Of course whether Western Christian civilization (in its religious and its secular form) is a good thing or not is for a higher tribunal than us to judge. Be that as it may, I think I have shown in the second section of this piece that scientific positivism of the kind espoused by Harris (and many others) excludes not only religion but a great swathe of our other reasonable beliefs as well and is for this reason too narrow to be convincing. Moreover, I think I have shown in the third section that religious beliefs that seem absurd as empirical propositions can seem perfectly sane and indeed foundational for a world civilization when considered from the standpoint of other forms of belief.

6 PINKER'S ENLIGHTENMENT

I recently read an article in the Huffington Post on religion and intelligence. Intelligence is so nebulous and so ideologically loaded a concept that it can seem scarcely worth discussing its relationship to anything. However, I did note one interesting feature of this article. While it is probably useless to attempt to define how 'intelligent' the average 'believer' is it does seem to be the case that intellectuals (who anyone who works in a university quickly realizes are no smarter than mechanics or rap artists) do tend on the whole to be more secular. One reason postulated for this fact is that 'intelligent' people or 'intellectuals' are unsatisfied with religion because they have stringent standards of evidence which can only be satisfied by the rigors of scientific method.[63] I will leave it to the reader to decide whether this has to do with any intrinsic quality of the 'intelligent' or rather with the ways in which they are socialized. I will also leave it to the reader to decide whether literary critics, who espouse opinions for which there is no conceivable scientific test, are to be classed as intelligent. I want to consider, briefly, how far this equation of science and its method with general intelligence can be pushed. Fortunately, I have an articulate partner in this discussion: Dr. Steven Pinker of Harvard University has recently written a spirited defense of science against those he thinks to be its enemies. In particular, he identifies science with the tradition of enlightenment which he feels has been subject to an unjust amount of criticism.[64]

---

[63]Macrina Cooper-White, "Religious People Branded as Less Intelligent than Atheists in Provocative New Study," *The Huffington Post*, August 14, 2013, http://www.huffingtonpost.com/2013/08/14/religious-people-less-intelligent-atheists_n_3750096.html

[64]Steven Pinker, "Science is Not Your Enemy: A Plea for an Intellectual Truce," *The New Republic*, August 19th 2013.

According to Pinker both the left and the right have perpetrated a negative image of science as the moving force behind the military, ecological and technical disasters of our century. Moreover, the hegemony of science is, these critics claim, at the heart of the moral vacuum that threatens our civilization. Quite rightly, Pinker rejects this stance. With perfect legitimacy he points out that science is indeed a moral enterprise with crucial values embedded within it. As Pinker points out, science embodies a commitment both to the hypothesis that the world is intelligible (and that intelligibility is preferable to its opposite) AND to the notion that uncovering the intelligible structures of the world is a task or discipline involving "...skepticism, open debate, formal precision and empirical tests...".[65] Thus, science both seeks something good in itself and encodes key intellectual values in its traditions and practices. In contrast, says Pinker, "...faith, revelation, dogma, authority, charisma, conventional wisdom, the invigorating glow of subjective certainty- are generators of error and should be dismissed as sources of knowledge".[66] Pinker concludes from this that "the moral world-view of any scientifically literate person...requires a radical break from religious conceptions of meaning and value".[67] This is because on crucial questions such as human origins the "traditional religions and cultures- their theories of the origins of life, humans, and societies- are factually mistaken".[68] Thus, the religious traditions about human origins are (with hats off to Popper again!) decisively falsified. Because of this, Pinker tells us, "...the worldview that guides the moral and spiritual values of an educated person today is the world given to us by science".[69] Moreover, religions, being factually in error about human origins, can claim no infallibility in matters of morality or values.[70]

At times, Pinker can come across as a naïve counter-fundamentalist. Any reader who goes through this book should (I hope) be long past worrying whether the great myths of the Greeks, Hebrews and Babylonians are factually true. That is not the sort of truth myths have, either for us or their original believers who were much more concerned that a story be sanctioned by authority than that it 'correspond' to 'facts' in the world. Anyone who now reads the book of *Genesis* can

---

[65] Pinker, "Science is Not Your Enemy."
[66] Pinker, "Science is Not Your Enemy."
[67] Pinker, "Science is Not Your Enemy."
[68] Pinker, "Science is Not Your Enemy."
[69] Pinker, "Science is Not Your Enemy."
[70] Pinker, "Science is Not Your Enemy."

easily see that it belongs to the genres of myth and saga and must be read and understood accordingly. Regarded as such it is as powerful and true as the *Illiad* or *Antigone*. Nor can I see why the great revelation of God as agape in the gospels rests on the factual inerrancy of their contents. Moreover, Pinker is surprisingly un-reconstructed in his attitude to science. I don't just refer here to his multiple references to Popper's now dated falsifiability principle. His praise of science takes no account of a problem even so basic as Hume's critique of induction. Thus, he cheerfully asserts that the intelligibility of the world can be inferred from the success of science though no legitimate inference can be drawn without assuming that intelligibility beforehand.[71] Moreover, Pinker contrasts science with other forms of knowing by calling the latter 'generators of error' which should be 'dismissed as sources of knowledge'. This is indeed an odd thing to say. Even the most scrupulous application of scientific method can still generate plenty of error for our data is always incomplete. Science is a proximate or local source of truth (not a necessary or inevitable one) but of course so are the modes of knowing dismissed by Pinker: no human can get through life without relying on conventional wisdom at some point, many great ideas appeared first in the form of a revelation or myth, almost all knowledge imparted in an elementary school rests on authority and the subjective glow of certainty can have excellent truth-making properties as any salesman knows.[72]

Of course, scientific knowledge, however incomplete, is also methodical and much more directly engages our reflective capacities than other more immediate forms of knowing. This is all to the good for examining and testing our thoughts is always desirable where it is possible. In this sense we should always, as Kant enjoins us 'dare to know'. However, we should pause, perhaps, to apply this principle to some of Pinker's own claims. Is it true for instance that the world-view of an educated person today is that of the sciences? Well, it certainly is in the sense that knowledge gleaned from the sciences should inform our outlook on the world. I am thankful when biologists or chemists or astronomers teach me something I would not otherwise have known.

---

[71]Pinker, "Science is Not Your Enemy." A strict empiricist could only say, at most, that science has worked up to this point. It could, after all, start a long string of failures tomorrow. Like Ptolomaic astronomy it may work reasonably well until it doesn't.

[72]William James made this point some time ago: "The desire for a certain kind of truth... brings about that truth's existence." ("The Will to Believe" in *Selected Papers on Philosophy*, 118)

However, I am not quite sure if this is what Pinker means. It sometimes seems that he is trying to make a grander claim than this: that the sciences are the chief bearers of the enlightenment and the chief field in which 'skepticism and open debate' are fostered. Being 'intelligent' (in the sense of intellectually responsible) would then equate with approaching the world as the natural sciences approach the world. If this is Pinker's meaning then I cannot possibly accept it as true. Obviously, the humane disciplines employ hermeneutical principles broader and more general than experimental testing and yet have no trouble producing knowledge of a kind and precision appropriate to them (i.e. well-informed opinions). I will grant though that it may not really be Pinker's intent to hold a position that flies so completely in the face of reality. I suspect that what he really wants to say is that whatever may belong with the natural sciences as part and parcel of the enlightenment world view, Religion is definitively excluded from it.

If this is so, Pinker's enlightenment is strangely disconnected from the actual historical enlightenment of which scientism and militant atheism were hardly prominent features (except on its fringes). Time after time we find Descartes, Locke, Kant, Spinoza, Galileo, Kepler, Newton, Leibniz, et. al. engaged deeply with the question of God and not in dismissive or derogatory ways either. One might further mention figures like Schliermacher or Lessing who engaged in theological reflection of a high order while fully committed to core enlightenment values. Whose enlightenment, then, are we talking about? Pinker is aware of the problem but answers it lamely. If only, he sighs, poor Descartes had possessed all the data we possess today on neuroscience! If only Leibniz or Kant had known about hormones! Surely they would have thrown their metaphysical-transcendental rubbish in the dust bin![73] This assumes falsely that the metaphysical and epistemological reflections of these thinkers were conditioned solely by the state of the natural sciences in their day. Kant, for instance, is thinking more about the conditions of the possibility of any science than he is of Newton or Galileo in particular. Descartes' third meditation on the existence of God may be right or wrong but it is not right or wrong based on any advance in physics or biology for the simple reason that Descartes is reflecting about God on a much for fundamental basis than the structure or nature of matter. He is engaged rather in full-blown metaphysics, that is, his reflections proceed under the most general categories of being and non-being. Leibniz thought that

---

[73] Pinker, "Science is Not Your Enemy."

the mechanical principles of the new physics were intrinsically limited (though valid in their domain) and needed to be supplemented by a deeper *metaphysical* reflection (his so called 'monadology'). None of them thought that the role of metaphysics was to make good the accidental failings of science: on the contrary, the most complete scientific account of the world possible would leave the most fundamental questions, such as the existence of God or the nature of consciousness, untouched. Pace Pinker the great thinkers of the enlightenment were intrinsically metaphysicians or philosophical theologians and there is no point in trying to rescue their reputations for modern secular humanists by pretending otherwise.

One cannot argue, then, that what is called natural theology or philosophy of religion is alien to the enlightenment. However, philosophical theology is not all of theology even as theology is not all of religion. Much theology, for instance, concerns the interpretation of doctrines founded in part or in whole on revealed scriptures. This, of course, raises the question of how we are to regard revealed religion from the standpoint of enlightenment. This is a problem I will consider briefly in the remainder of this essay. One way I can approach it is by reflecting on the role 'skepticism and open dialogue' play in a religious attitude to the world. Of course, this is problematic for authority seems to play such a role in the constitution of religious institutions that it may seem impossible to reconcile them with the full demands of enlightenment. Skepticism and open debate have certainly occurred in the history of religion (Pinker could not possibly be so ill-informed as to think otherwise) yet it seems that they are ever destined to lose out to a greater principle, that of authority, whether this be of the clergy or scripture, which, perhaps, is why it seems so noxious to Dr. Pinker. Yet authority has its place in the sciences too. Indeed, it has its place in any human endeavor. In fact, I think science is one realm where authority functions rather effectively and humanely (on the whole) and that religion (in particular) can learn some useful lessons from it.

Skepticism and debate are one aspect of science that Dr. Pinker certainly over-emphasizes. While they are welcome inside science they are only admitted on a localized and well-defined terrain. Few disciplines guard their borders as fiercely and husband their gains as carefully as the sciences do. This is because each one of the sciences is an institutional structure and a form of life before it is anything else. This structure embodies certain examples or paradigms of good scientific practice that act as a kind of check on individual eccentricity or caprice. Science is a collective endeavor first and foremost and every scientist is responsible not only to his own conscience but to the expectations and values of his colleagues as well. A refusal to play within the rules of the science game results in banishment from the scientific community: as happens to astrologers, creationists or individual cranks like Immanuel Velikovsky or Wilhelm Reich. One of the positive things about science is that scientific heresy, unlike religious heresy, usually results in ruined reputations rather than ruined limbs. However, the principle is the same: the integrity of the institution of science demands adherence to certain fundamental values encoded in the practice of the various disciplines and failure to do this will lead to sanction. The authority that imposes sanction resides in hiring committees, granting agencies, department heads and peer review journals. It cannot, like many religious bodies can, call upon the coercive power of the state (except in rare circumstances- such as the case of Reich) yet if anything this has made scientific authority more and not less effective.

In this respect, scientific institutions are much like religious ones. As scientists accept the basic data of experience, theologians accord the same status to the scriptures or religious traditions of which they present themselves as interpreters. As much as in the sciences this interpretation is subject to control by certain paradigms of good theology, sometimes enshrined in dogmatic definitions, sometimes in canonical authors such as Aquinas or Calvin and sometimes in long-standing tradition. Anyone who falls afoul of this paradigm, for instance by being grossly one-sided on some basic question of theology, is of course, subject to sanction by the community, exactly as in the sciences. However, here I note an interesting difference. No doubt because religion has been tied up with basic moral and social values in a way more intense and involved than the sciences there has been a tendency to go much farther in policing dissent than physicists and biologists would ever want or need to do. Moreover, religion has failed at this where the sciences have more or less succeeded. For all Pinker's talk of open debate, there is probably more unanimity of opinion in a chemistry department than in a conclave of cardinals. We have many religions but we do not have many bodies of science: in the field of religion a 'heresy' can break off and become its own orthodoxy with its own canons of interpretation and its own paradigms of theological excellence. These new communities will, of course, have debates and strife over a range of 'open' issues while maintaining unanimity on those issues that are more fundamental and therefore 'closed'. In this they will not differ appreciably from the sciences: it would be impossible to debate any issue in chemistry if there were not some measure of consensus on what issues were live and what issues were dead. It would be a lamentable waste of time to begin first year chemistry with the controversy over phlogiston!

Now it sounds like I have made both religion and science out to be essentially conservative institutions in which debate about some ideas is only possible through suppression of debate about others. In this respect neither religion nor science belong properly to Pinker's enlightenment. If Pinker wants open debate and skepticism full bore he should perhaps look in the direction of Paul Feyerabend and his epistemological anarchism. Yet I do not yet think we have gotten to the last word on this subject for science and religion do have their revolutionary phases as well. From the time of Constantine to the papacy of Hildebrand (Gregory VII) to the second Vatican Council the Roman Catholic church has undergone a series of revolutionary transformations. The many Protestant denominations have their origin in the great reformation of the 16th century. Judaism underwent a 19th century reform that remains vital to this day and transformations of consciousness are occurring as we speak in the Islamic tradition. In the sciences we have seen the revolutionary element at work in Copernicus, Einstein and Neils Bohr. At these times, historians like Kuhn have taught us, fundamental questions about the nature of science itself are 'up for grabs' and controversy can rage over the broadest range of issues. Thus, whether we speak of the sciences or of the churches assertions of orthodoxy co-exist in tension with revolutionary movements of the spirit.

Here is where I suggest we can find the core of an enlightened attitude. The enlightenment does not divide over the question of science and religion. Both are inexpugnably part of our world as much as they were part of the world of Descartes or Kant. Enlightenment's true concern is surely with how we are to be religious and how we are to be scientific. What it is to be enlightened about religion is perhaps something still in the process of being defined. However, I think I can say what it is to be unenlightened about it. This is to assume a defensive stance that seeks to reinforce boundaries as they now exist. With the burgeoning consciousness of a global culture we are in a revolutionary time for religion and the calling of all religious people is to rise to this challenge and regard the total spiritual patrimony of human-kind as in some sense its own heritage. This is precisely what fundamentalisms of various kinds refuse to do. It involves not only the embrace of alien traditions such as Buddhism or Sufism but the embrace of the arts, philosophy and science as well. To be wisely religious is to know we live in an age of revolution and not in an age of consolidation or construction (such as, say, Benedict of Nursia or Gregory the Great lived in). To be wisely religious is to know that what is hollow or faddish will die its own death but that what comes from the spirit cannot be opposed.

We should remember too that contrary to what Pinker asserts science is not coterminous with enlightenment. For one thing, there are centuries of science that pre-date it. Moreover, science can be practiced under totalitarian regimes as well as enlightened liberal ones. The question then would be: what is an enlightened attitude in science? Perhaps this is also something we are in the process of defining. Certainly, it is unenlightened to apply scientific modes of knowing outside the domains with which science is concerned. It is unenlightened to regard the pursuit of the scientific progress to be an absolute imperative that overrides fundamental humanity: the sciences were made for humankind not humankind for the sciences. Nor is it enlightened for the sciences to assume that the form they have taken in the modern West is absolute and fixed: closed to the contributions of non-Western traditions, indigenous knowledges or the contributions of women or other excluded groups. Defensive assertions of the hegemony of instrumental reason that are thinly veiled calls for the restoration of a vanished Anglo-American imperialism (as in writers like the late Christopher Hitchens) are doomed from the start and any defender of the Western version of enlightenment must bow to this fundamental fact. As in religion, an enlightened scientific community is one which is prepared to serve the cause of human development rather than retreat behind a wall of entrenched professionalism. In other words, an enlightened person is not one who is religious or scientific. An enlightened person is one who is intelligently religious or scientific. Enlightenment is not a dogmatic assertion of scientific method or instrumental reason. Enlightenment is an attitude to life or a form of wisdom. Perhaps its basic moral stance can be summed up in the dictum of Terence: "nothing human is alien to me".

7 A NOTE ON TRUTH

To conclude this book I would like to say a few words about truth. Richard Dawkins is a man who not only knows the truth but claims to know what sort of thing truth is. Indeed, he has a little talk on truth which he thought worthy of preservation in a collection of his essays, and it is worthy of presentation for he gives us his exact opinion on the matter. Let me quote: "It is simply true that the sun is hotter than the earth, true that the desk on which I am writing is made of wood...It is forever true that DNA is a double helix, true that if you and a chimpanzee (or an octopus or a kangaroo) trace your ancestors back far enough you will eventually hit a shared ancestor...".[74] Moreover, Dawkins assures us that "these are not hypotheses awaiting falsification; not temporary approximations to an ever elusive truth; not truths that might be denied in another culture", and continues with: "...these statements are true in exactly the same sense as the ordinary truths of life; true in the same sense as it is true that you have a head, and that my desk is wooden".[75] This is admirably clear: truth, any truth, is simple fact. Truth is an attribute of propositions that state what is the case correctly. This may seem too obvious to state but Dawkins feels he must remind us about truth lest we be taken in by two pernicious sorts of people: 'truth hecklers' in philosophy of science and 'cultural relativists' in sociology, anthropology and Women's studies. The first group claim that scientific propositions are only provisionally true in the sense that they have not yet been falsified. The second group claim that science is only one truth among many, it is a Western sort of truth no more and no less valid than

---

[74]Richard Dawkins, "What is True" in *The Devil's Chaplain* (Boston: Haughton Mifflin Co., 2004), 239.
[75]Dawkins, "What is True," 239.

Kikuyu truth, Navaho truth or 'Bongolese' truth.[76] Some of these
thinkers even claim that Western science is in fact 'male' science and
hence not necessarily true from the perspective of women.

To both these groups Dawkins has the same answer: science, he
tells us, is true because of its results – it makes true predictions we can
rely on practically and much of the technology on which we depend is
simply applied science.[77] This is an interesting claim on Dawkins' part
for it reflects a different view of truth than that laid out above: it is a
pragmatic or instrumental view of truth. One could, of course, argue
that instrumental truth 'works' because it is grounded on 'common
sense factual truth'. Alas, Dawkins gives no argument as to why this is
so. Perhaps he regards it as an obvious proposition but it is nothing of
the kind. The instrumental and the factual can and do diverge. Even
today accurate and useful predictions can be made using the Ptolomaic
model of the solar system even though no one regards it as 'factually'
true. Indeed, Dawkins himself recognizes that quantum mechanics is
instrumentally successful even though the claims it makes are scarcely
comprehensible as 'ordinary facts'. It is hard not to conclude then
that Dawkins is operating with *two* conceptions of truth which he has
naively conflated.

Now in these essays I have been trying to articulate a rather different sense of truth. I have no problem with realists and instrumentalists
per se except that I think their positions incomplete: there are, as we
have seen in the previous essay, many truths that do not correspond
to facts and are not simply instrumental. In aesthetics for instance,
we make judgments that correspond not to facts but to an *intelligible
standard*, in this case the idea of beauty (however we happen to determine it). Indeed, one might say that after all is said and done 'true'
may have the sense of 'true to' at its foundation. The statement 'the
beer is in the fridge' conforms to the standard of correct reportage.
Similarly, the statement 'the assassination of Martin Luther King was
a crime' conforms to the idea of justice as to a standard. Similarly,
the statement 'Darwin's theory of evolution is true' means that it con-

---

[76]The Bongolese, Dawkins informs us, have a concept of 'in' according to which
"...you are only truly 'in' a place if you are an anointed elder entitled to take snuff
from the dried scrotum of a goat" (*What is True,* p. 239). So far I have not been
able to discover who these 'Bongolese' are. I sincerely hope they are not a racist
caricature invented by Dawkins in a clumsy stab at humor. Alas, as several of the
examples he uses in this essay reek of contempt for indigenous cultures I fear they
may be just that.
[77]Dawkins, "What is True," 237.

forms to the standard we expect of a good theory, i.e. it is reasonably accurate as a reflection of the data, is parsimonious, is fruitful in terms of the development of further research, etc.[78]

This brings me to the question of what truth in religion might be and whether we can ever be justified in saying that we have found it. I do not raise this question in the old-fashioned sense of asking which, among all the world's faiths, is demonstrably true. Those who want to pursue that question are welcome to though I fear that their inquiry may yield a meager crop. If one is a Christian, as the present author is, one should reflect that calling Christianity 'the true religion' is ass-backward. Jesus Christ is the truth of any Christian faith as he is of any other human phenomenon and indeed of any other faith deeply and authentically lived. It is the person of the savior that counts and not the historical entity we call Christendom (with its various denominations) and certainly not a list of propositions that we regard as *de fide*. However, reflecting a bit on the figure of Jesus, let's see if we can approach the question of truth in religion from another angle. What is 'truth' in religion 'true to'? We can find a surprising amount on this question in the *Gospel of John* for throughout Jesus is appealing to the precise sense of truth I am articulating here.

On more than one occasion I have used John's gospel as an introductory text in a great books course. The students, looking at it for the first time as a text and not as a religious artifact, are quite rightly puzzled. Jesus speaks in large abstractions. He speaks of truth, of freedom, of life, of goodness, of love, yet rarely does he stop and explain these words. Often he is maddeningly indirect, answering questions with parables, with short aphoristic statements or even with a riddling question of his own. Yet he claims to come with a revelation from the Father; he claims to speak the truth by speaking the words his father has given him. Yet again the truth he brings is obviously not a set of propositions or statements of fact. On this level Jesus says little that is clear and direct so that even his closest followers are in the dark about what he means. Yet still this riddling fellow Jesus claims to be the 'light of the world.'

How is this so? I cannot, of course, give a comprehensive answer here. However, I can make a few suggestions based on my own reading of the text. Firstly, truth in *John* concerns propositional or factual

---

[78]It is interesting to note that if a theory is to be fruitful it *cannot* in fact be too accurate. For research to progress a theory must generate puzzles and anomalies for researchers to work on. This is why Feyerabend says, with what is perhaps characteristic exaggeration, that *every* good theory is contradicted by the facts.

statements only in a secondary and derivative sense. Jesus persistently demands that his hearers recognize the truth which is freedom and eternal life. This is a truth which is manifested in action. Jesus *does* the deeds of his Father and in doing so *does* the truth. Anyone who in turn follows Jesus in what he does follows the Father. As he says: "Believe me that I am in the Father, and the Father in me: or else believe me for the very works' sake. Verily, Verily I say onto you, He that believeth in me, the works that I do he shall also do; and greater works than these shall he do; because I go onto my Father".[79] This is not a claim to any sort of magical infallibility. Jesus persistently denies that he is any kind of witness to himself. Rather, his deeds being those of the Father, he manifests the nature of the Father. What is the nature of the Father? Jesus says it is a*gape* or unconditional love. Thus, his charge to his disciples, his only direct charge, is that they manifest to others the *agape* of the Father as he has manifested it to them: "If ye keep my commandments ye shall abide in my love; even as I have kept my Father's commandments and abide in his love... This is my commandment, that ye love one another as I have loved you".[80] This *agape* or unconditional love is most completely and fully manifested as sacrificial love so that "greater love hath no man than to lay down his life for his friends".[81] Thus, they are to show to each other this sacrificial love of the Father as he has revealed it and constitute thus the Kingdom of God, a community founded on mutual and unconditional love of neighbour.

How do I know that what Jesus demands is the truth? The question is a valid one and is posed by Pontius Pilate at Jesus' trial. Jesus' implied response (he does not give a discursive answer to the question) is the light of his own actions. The true, as a radiance of the good, shines forth from what is done in truth. The deeds of Jesus illuminate themselves: they are their own light and radiate their own truth. In that sense they resemble the beauty of a work of art. But of course *all* deeds of love have this self-illuminating character: they are directly *seen* as good by those who are prepared to recognize them (as many, blinded by egotism, fear and pride, are not). Indeed, the experience of charity, if one has it, is a self-authenticating one. The man rescued by the Good Samaritan needs no long disquisition on ethics to see the nature of what has occurred: one act of charity has profoundly altered

---

[79] *John* 14, 11-12. See also *John* 13, 34-35.
[80] *John* 15, 10-12.
[81] *John* 15, 13.

a human situation. A barrier assumed as absolute has been broken and a new freedom to act obtained. After true love has manifested in this way there is no going back to the old exclusions as the new revelation of *agape* has rendered them simply irrelevant. A 'brave new world' has come into being.

Augustine argued in his great work *On Christian Doctrine* that *agape* or for him *caritas* was the ultimate principle of theological hermeneutics. What any text, or any doctrine or any law had to be true to in order to be true was the demand of love. On this basis, Augustine argued that any interpretation of any difficult biblical text had to edify or build up charity.[82] Insofar as the scriptures have the character of human documents they of course have much in them that is extraneous, crude and ultimately contingent. Yet even these texts can be elevated and indeed redeemed by the mind inflamed by love of God and neighbour. This was elaborated by Augustine into a practice of symbolic and allegorical reading which could bring the best out of any scriptural text. Many of the details of Augustine's symbolic readings may now seem strained but as a method of dealing with sacred texts I am not sure they have been surpassed. However this may be, I would simply note here that for Augustine, as for Jesus, truth in religion is the word of love and this is the ultimate measure of truth in religion and, I do not hesitate to affirm, of truth simply. Charity, I hold, is the truth of any science (Nazi science or any science that serves exclusion or hate is false in more than a propositional sense). Indeed, it is the truth of any art or philosophy one cares to name insofar as all these things, when they are doing what they ought, serve the earthly reign of love. This, I hope, is a truth we might all agree upon.

---

[82] *On Christian Doctrine*, 39.

References

Aquinas *Summa of Theology* (Chicago: Encyclopedia Britannica Inc., 1952)

Aristotle *Metaphysics* trans. R. McKeon (NewYork:Random House, 1941)

Aristotle *Nichomachean Ethics* trans. R. McKeon (NewYork:Random House, 1941)

Aristotle *Poetics* trans. R. McKeon(NewYork:Random House, 1941)

Augustine *The City of God* trans.H. Bettenson (London: Penguin Classics, 1984)

Augustine *On Christian Doctrine* trans. D.W. Robertson (New York: Macmillan, 1958)

Augustine *Confessions* trans. H. Chadwick (Oxford: Oxford University Press, 1992)

Barbour, Ian. *Religion in an Age of Science.* San Francisco: Harper & Row, 1990.

The Church Teaches (Rockford: Tan Books and Publishers, 1973)

Cole, Stuart G. *The History of Fundamentalism* (Westport: Greenwood Press, 1971)

Cooper-White, Macrina "Religious People Branded as Less Intelligent than Atheists in Provocative New Study," The Huffington Post, August 14, 2013, http://www.huffingtonpost.com/2013/08/14/religious-people-less-intelligent-atheists_n_3750096.html

Cornwell, John *Darwin's Angel: An Angelic Riposte to* The God Delusion. London: Profile Books, 2007.

Cumont, Franz *Astrology among the Greeks and Romans* (NewYork: G.P. Putnam and Sons, 1912)

Dawkins, Richard. *The God Delusion.* Boston: Houghton Mifflin Co., 2006.

—. "What is True." *The Devil's Chaplain* (Boston: Houghton Mifflin Harcourt, 2004)

Eagleton, Terry "Lunging Flailing and Mis-punching." *London Review of Books* 28, no. 20 (2006): 32-34.

Eriugena, *Periphuseon* (Montreal: Editions Bellarmin, 1987)

Feyerabend, Paul K "How to Defend Society Against Science." *Full Poster* (2008) http://www.fullposter.com/snippets.php?snippet=310

Flew, Anthony "Theology and Falsification." In *New Essays in Philosophical Theology.* Edited by Anthony Flew and Alasdair Mac-

Intyre, 267-268. London: SCM Press, 1955.

Frye, Northrop *The Great Code* Toronto: Academia Press, 1982.

Gadamer, H. G. *Truth and Method.* New York: Seabury Press, 1975.

Galileo, *Dialogue concerning the Two Chief World Systems* trans. Stillman Drake (1967: University of California Press, 328)

Gospel of John, The Holy Bible (New York: Thomas Nelson Inc. 1977)

Hare, R. M. "Response to Anthony Flew." In *New Essays in Philosophical Theology.* Edited by Anthony Flew and Alasdair MacIntyre, 268-269. London: SCM Press, 1955.

Harris, Errol E. *Atheism and Theism* (New Orleans: Tulane university, 1977)

Harris, Sam *The End of Faith: Religion, Terror, and the Future of Reason.* New York: W. W. Norton & Co., 2005.

Heraclitus *Early Greek Philosophy* trans. Jonathan Barnes (Penguin Classics, New York, 1987)

Hesse, Mary *Models and Analogies in Science.* Notre Dame: University of Notre Dame Press, 1970.

Kuhn, Thomas *The Structure of Scientific Revolutions* (Chicago: University of Chicago Press, 1996)

James, William "The Will to Believe" *Selected Papers on Philosophy* (London: Everyman, 1943)

Jung, Carl Gustav "Instinct and the Unconscious" in *The Portable Jung* ed. Joseph Campbell (London: Penguin Books, 1976)

Laudan, Larry (1983) "The Demise of the Demarcation Problem, In Robert S. Cohen & Larry Laudan (eds.), *Physics, Philosophy and Psychoanalysis: Essays in Honor of Adolf Grünbaum.* D. Reidel, Dordrecht, Netherlands. 111—127.

Lindberg, David C. *The Beginnings of Western Science: The European Scientific Tradition in Philosophical, Religious, and Institutional Context, Prehistory to A.D. 1450.* Chicago: Chicago University Press, 2007.

Lakatos, Imre "Science and Pseudo-Science", http://www.lse.ac.uk/philosophy/department-history/science-and-pseudoscience-BBC, 1973. Overview-and-transcript, Retrieved Feb. 25, 2015.

James Livingston and Francis Schlusser Fiorenza *Modern Christian Thought* Vol.2 (Upper Saddle River: Prentice Hall, 2000)

Ursula LaGuin *The Dispossessed* (New York: Harper Voyager, 1994)

Lonergan, Bernard *The Road to Nicea.* (London: Darton,Longman & Todd Ltd, 1976)

Longino, Helen "Feminism and Philosophy of Science": http://onlinelibrary.wiley.com/doi/10.1111/j.1467-9833.1990.tb00287.x/pd

Marcel, Gabriel *Being and Having.* Translated by Katharine Farrer. Westminster: Dacre Press, 1949.

McGrath, Alister. *Introduction to Christianity.* Oxford: Blackwell Publishers, 1997.

De la Mirandola, Pico *Oration on the Dignity of Man, The Renaissance Philosophy of Man* ed. Kristeller, Cassirer and Randall (Chicago: University of Chicago Press, 1948)

Newman, John Henry *An Essay in Aid of a Grammar of Assent.* London: Burns & Oates, 1881.

Pinker, Steven "Science is Not Your Enemy: A Plea for an Intellectual Truce," *The New Republic*, August 19th 2013, http://www.lexisnexis.com.qe2a-proxy.mun.ca/hottopics/lnacademic/?verb=sr&csi=154997&sr=HLEAD(Science%20is%20not%20your%20enemy)%20and%20date%20is%202013

Pelikan, Jaroslav *The Emergence of the Catholic Tradition* (Chicago: University of Chicago Press, 1971)

Plato *The Republic, Collected Dialogues* ed. Hamilton and Cairns (Princeton: Princeton University Press, 1971)

Polanyi, Michael *The Tacit Dimension* (Chicago: University of Chicago Press, 2009)

Popper, Karl R. *Conjectures and Refutations: The Growth of Scientific Knowledge.* New York: Harper & Row, 1968.

Quine, W. V. O. "Two Dogmas of Empiricism." In *From a Logical Point of View* (Harvard University Press, 1961), http://www.ditext.com/quine/quine.html

Rosenberg, Alexander *The Atheist's Guide to Reality.* New York: W. W. Norton, 2011.

Salmon, Wesley "The Problem of Induction" (Philosophical Studies vol.33 no. 1, 1978).

Sayers, Dorothy L. "Scalene Trinities." In *Mind of the Maker*, 119-144. London: Continuum International Publishing, 1994.

Smith, Graeme *A Short History of Secularism* (London: IB Tauris, 2008)

About the author

Bernard Wills is professor of Humanities at Grenfell Campus Memorial University. He has an M.A. in Classics from Dalhousie University and a PH.D. in Religious Studies from McMaster University. He received his B.A. from University of King's College where he conceived his lifelong interest in classical and early Christian thought. His teaching, like his research, ranges from popular culture (he has written on Cohen and is working on Dylan) to the history of Platonism in Early Modern Europe. His poetry has appeared in *The Antigonish Review*, *Vallum* and *Papermill Press*. He resides in Corner Brook NL. with his wife Jean and his three sons. He also has an (all grown up!) daughter.